Communication is EVERYTHING in my business. I am so excited for this book to be an extra tool for those (like me) who need it.

—**Whitney Reynolds,** Emmy nominated PBS talk show host,
Whitney Reynolds Show

I read *Communication Essentials* in one weekend. This gem of a book is loaded with wisdom and practical insights that are immediately useful today, although I wish I had been handed it a decade ago!

—**Charles Leddy,** Chief Executive Officer,
Presidian Hotels & Resorts

Dr. Guinn's book covers the foundations and principles of communication, along with practical examples and scenarios that are widely applicable to the modern workplace. Be sure to read this short and compact guide that will help you take your communication skills to the next level!

—**Dr. Doris Lee,** Cofounder and CEO, Ponder

No matter who you are or how you spend your days, Dr. Guinn convincingly argues that communication skills are a nonnegotiable essential to healthy friendships, supervisory relationships, one's leadership capacity, or any professional endeavor. This thoughtful book is teeming with practical tips and wise counsel that I immediately deployed.

—**Dr. Frank Shushok,** President, Roanoke College

When you think about the essentials in any subject, you want to be taught by your favorite professor or the best coach you've ever had. Dr. Guinn is both of those in one, and he will help you master the communication essentials in such a way that you'll be amazed at what you learned, how effective you can become, and how much fun it was to do so.

—**Dr. Dub Oliver,** President, Union University

Knowing your audience is the easy part. Knowing how to successfully communicate with that audience is the difficult part. Dr. Guinn has delivered a book loaded with insight and offers actionable takeaways to help a person develop and grow as an effective communicator.

—**Charles A. Gonzalez,** Former US Representative and
Texas State District Judge

A comprehensive self-help guide to communicating, Dr. Guinn's book leads you through the elements of communication, why it's important to communicate effectively, and provides practical tools you can use to improve your own messaging. This is an excellent read for the young professional, seasoned senior management, and anyone in between, including those wanting to simply improve their personal relationships!

—**John McPherson,** Major, United States Air Force

Communication Essentials is a special book which has changed the way I communicate and lead. Dr. Guinn's human-centered lessons and applied framework will help a lot of people lead more successful lives.

—**Dan Peng**, Product Manager, Google

If *How to Win Friends and Influence People* was the most famous effective communication skills book of the twentieth century, *Communication Essentials* will likely be the effective communication classic of our generation. This is the book I wish I had 20 years ago, and I am happy that I have it today. I look forward to sharing it with my coworkers, friends, and family.

—**Korhan Bircan**, Director of Engineering, Square

Every human who interacts with other humans should read this book! Dr. Guinn has successfully combined his years of teaching, research, and coaching into an engaging and insightful text that meets individuals wherever they are. An outstanding book from an exceptional and dynamic expert in human communication.

—**Dr. Sarah Varga**, Baylor University

A must-read for those ready to unlock a higher level of professional impact. This book will shape how I approach the next chapter of my career.

—**Kimberly Fransham**, Senior Associate Brand Manager, General Mills

This book is what you need to uplevel your communication!

—**Alex Magginetti**, Product Management, Microsoft

Dr. Guinn brilliantly coaches his reader to success by simultaneously demonstrating how to effectively communicate through his writing and examples and by providing digestible tips and frameworks. This book is a must-read for anyone seeking greater authenticity, impact, and effectiveness in their abilities to communicate, listen, and engage.

>—**Dr. Kristin Saboe,** Industrial-Organizational Psychologist and
>Senior HR Leader, Boeing

In *Communication Essentials*, Dr. Guinn portrays his charisma and eloquence in words. This book provides a fresh approach to communication frameworks while making the information easy to read. I would recommend this book to anyone looking to improve their communication skills to advance their career.

>—**Rodrigo Landivar,** Strategy Consultant, Accenture

There are very few books which give you specific actions to follow to improve the most important life skills to accelerate your career in this highly competitive environment. A must-read for everyone who wants to create an edge for themselves in today's fast changing corporate world.

>—**Vikas Prasad,** Head Consulting Sales—India,
>Amazon Web Services

This book is essential for anyone looking to communicate and connect more clearly in business and life. I can't wait to share this book with everyone I know!

>—**Hannah Halff,** Corporate Strategy, Nordstrom

Whether you are an awesome communicator or someone who's looking to improve your communications, this is the perfect book for you! Dr. Guinn's book has the power to connect and inspire people to build confidence in their communication no matter what stage you are at in your career.

> —**Carol Lee**, Head of Global Compliance, Intuit

To build and strengthen our communication skills is to ultimately unlock power within ourselves to propel us forward in life when we feel stuck or ineffective. I promise you, reading *Communication Essentials* is an imperative investment toward your foundation and will enhance your life personally and professionally.

> —**Kali Rae Kirkpatrick**, New York Region Zone Manager,
> Ford Motor Company

Dr. Guinn has given us all a gift in this book—a gift for improved relationships, lasting friendships, a soaring meaningful career, and an overall good life. You will help yourself for life by reading *Communication Essentials* and absorbing all the advice Dr. Guinn provides.

> —**D. F.**, Senior Technical Program Manager, Meta and former
> Global Strategy Consultant, Samsung

Communication Essentials reads like a friend sitting down with you over coffee, exploring how communication skills influence every part of our lives. Dr. Guinn will help you see communication not as an abstract theory, but a lifelong journey of better understanding ourselves and others.

> —**Dr. Gary Guadagnolo**, PhD, Director of Research Strategy, EAB

The perfect book for anyone eager to work on their overall communication skills and ready to start an eye-opening journey of self-reflection. Dr. Guinn not only provides very practical advice on how to improve communication, both at a professional and personal level, but he also guides the reader to understand all nonverbal aspects of communication and how they affect our relationships with ourselves and others in all areas of life.

> —**Yndra Hurtado de la Llata,** Global Partner Integration, Dell
> Technologies

Communication Essentials is a gift to our world. This book flows like a river of joy into all our hearts, showing us how to be kind, kind with others, and kind to ourselves.

> —**Carmen Raicu,** Sales Operations Leader, Hewlett-Packard

Dr. Guinn's hands-on frameworks and advice are priceless. A new job, a promotion, catchy pitches leading to more sales, or just better executive presence? It's mainly about how you communicate. Highly recommendable if you want to increase your communication skills and confidence within a couple of days!

> —**Dr. Mathias Hentrich,** Senior Manager, Accenture Strategy
> (Germany)

As a young leader who aspires to inspire my team and deepen my professional network, *Communication Essentials* has been my golden resource. Dr. Guinn's step-by-step approach has made me a more effective communicator to the team I lead, and has aided me in developing new professional network inroads to my next promotion. Highly recommend for those looking to improve life's most essential skill, communication!

> —**Justin Brown,** Business Manager, Bayer

Being an effective communicator is an important tool for creating success in life. Whether you're looking to build strong relationships or just enhance your professional communication skills, this book is a must-read for all ages!

—**Chris Cho**, Communications Director, NuStar Energy

Communication Essentials is truly essential in continuing the lifelong journey of improving a vital skill (communications) that makes the toughest conversations in any setting manageable.

—**Afreen Isaac**, Supply Demand Management, Apple

Dr. Guinn does a masterful job creating a modern and valuable handbook for arguably the most important skill in driving any successful outcome: communication! Just when you think you already know this stuff, *Communication Essentials* hits you with powerful, research-based insights you can immediately implement in your personal and professional life.

—**James Harper**, 20-year technology marketing veteran, B2B Saas marketing executive, former Amazon Web Services Lead Marketing Manager

Communication Essentials is an engaging three-part guide that utilizes personal anecdotes to lay out the framework necessary for successful and effective communication.

—**Dr. Jerry Fan**, Cardiologist, Baylor Scott & White Health—Temple

A great informative read that has caused me to think about how I'm communicating with the world around me. The concrete steps listed to help effectively communicate are extremely beneficial, and I will apply these going forward. Highly recommended!

—**Matt Tovar**, Senior Animation Engineer, *Uneeq*

Dr. Guinn is a true master of communication. I'm delighted that he is sharing his thinking and methods in this book so that many more can benefit from his guidance.

> —**Janet Rhines McIntyre,** ECommerce Innovation Marketing Manager, PepsiCo

What a prescriptive and applicable book across all life stages. Love that the essentials are weaved throughout and creating pathways for communication success!

> —**Sherry Zeng-Fargas,** Manager of Sales Planning, Amplify Snack Brands (The Hershey Company)

Effective communication is like any other skill—if you don't consistently and intentionally hone it, you'll lose it. I highly recommend this book for anyone looking to improve their communication mindset.

> —**Matt Johnson,** Assistant United States Attorney

This is a great book for teaching a framework for effective communication. The principles in this book will help you present your message as effectively as possible.

> —**Joe Aviles,** Business System Analyst, Google

This book is the communications how-to manual.

> —**Kyle Heisler,** Amazon

Throughout this book, Guinn provides actionable tips and suggestions on how to become a better communicator as well as real-life success stories. This book is for anyone who wants to become a more highly effective communicator and leader.

> —**Dr. Deidra Stephens,** Director of Texas McCombs+ Global & Experiential Learning, The University of Texas at Austin

COMMUNICATION
ESSENTIALS

THE TOOLS YOU NEED TO MASTER EVERY TYPE OF PROFESSIONAL INTERACTION

TREY GUINN

Mc
Graw
Hill

NEW YORK CHICAGO SAN FRANCISCO ATHENS LONDON
MADRID MEXICO CITY MILAN NEW DELHI
SINGAPORE SYDNEY TORONTO

1 2 3 4 5 6 7 8 9   LCR   27 26 25 24 23 22

ISBN 978-1-264-27805-3
MHID   1-264-27805-5

e-ISBN 978-1-264-27806-0
e-MHID   1-264-27806-3

Design by Mauna Eichner and Lee Fukui

Library of Congress Cataloging-in-Publication Data

Names: Guinn, Trey, author.
Title: Communication essentials : the tools you need to master every type
   of professional interaction / Trey Guinn.
Description: 1 Edition. | New York City : McGraw Hill, [2023] | Includes
   bibliographical references and index.
Identifiers: LCCN 2022035747 (print) | LCCN 2022035748 (ebook) | ISBN
   9781264278053 (paperback) | ISBN 9781264278060 (ebook)
Subjects: LCSH: Business communication. | Communication in organizations. |
   Communication and technology. | Interpersonal communication.
Classification: LCC HF5718 .G85 2023 (print) | LCC HF5718 (ebook) | DDC
   658.4/5—dc23/eng/20220728
LC record available at https://lccn.loc.gov/2022035747
LC ebook record available at https://lccn.loc.gov/2022035748

McGraw Hill books are available at special quantity discounts to use as premiums and sales promotions or for use in corporate training programs. To contact a representative, please visit the Contact Us pages at www.mhprofessional.com.

McGraw Hill is committed to making our products accessible to all learners. To learn more about the available support and accommodations we offer, please contact us at accessibility@mheducation.com. We also participate in the Access Text Network (www.accesstext.org), and ATN members may submit requests through ATN.

This book is dedicated to you.

Thanks for reading and joining me on this learning journey!

Contents

Preface   vii

Acknowledgments   ix

PART I
THE ESSENTIALS

1   **Be a Communication Student for Life**   3

2   **Know Why and How We Communicate**   15

3   **Discover the "I" in Communicate**   25

4   **Understand That the Message Sent Is Not Always the Message Received**   35

5   **Commit to Being Effective**   41

PART II
THE ESSENTIALS APPLIED

Communication Self-Assessment   51

6   **Your Communication Starting Point: Be Willing**   55

7   **Identify Your GOAL**   69

8   **Know Your AUDIENCE**   **79**

9   **Own Your MESSAGE**   **97**

10 **Anticipate How Your Audience
Will Perceive You, the MESSENGER**   **121**

11 **Choose the Best MEDIUM for Your Message**   **141**

PART III
BEYOND THE ESSENTIALS

12 **Communicate Your Way into a Job**   **155**

13 **Communicate on the Job and Up the Ladder**   **177**

14 **Improve Your Digital Communication**   **203**

15 **Communicate to Make and
Maintain Social Relationships**   **215**

16 **Communicate Through Conflict and
Difficult Conversations**   **227**

17 **Continue Learning to Keep Improving**   **251**

  Notes   **257**

  Index   **259**

Preface

No matter how broadly my professional network expands, what I observe about humans and how we can enhance our communication effectiveness remains mostly constant. From the first-generation college student in a speech course to the university president rehearsing a commencement address. From the MBA student preparing for interviews to the senior product manager prepping for a difficult conversation, and from the physician who is developing a bedside manner to the CEO prepping for the next earnings call. The faces change, the situations are unique, but important for each of us is understanding and learning to master the communication essentials.

If you are looking for a list of fast facts, search the internet and you will find many sources wrapped in clickbait waiting for you. But be forewarned, mastering communication doesn't work like that. Instead, communication is kind of like running. You can't read a web page on running and then win the Boston Marathon. You have to dig deep and do the work. Fortunately, the work can be fun.

If you're looking for an engaging book that's designed to support you on the pathway toward enhancing your communication effectiveness, you've come to the right place. This book has been written for you, no matter your age, location, or vocation.

In Part I, "The Essentials," I invite you to explore essential elements of communication and to be introspective with yourself as a communicator. In Part II, "The Essentials Applied," I provide an easy-to-remember framework for how to apply and eventually master the communication essentials. In Part III, "Beyond the Essentials," I give pro tips for navigating a variety of professional communication scenarios.

Let's get started.

Acknowledgments

My kids will tell you that my most frequently said phrase is, "Guinns are grateful." To no surprise, I feel enormous gratitude writing and publishing this book. I am thankful for the process and to the many individuals who helped me along the way. My list of "thank yous" is quite long because the content of this book is not only the result of a recently finished project but also a collection of insights discovered, rediscovered, and refined over a lifetime. My own life experiences, including years of study, teaching, and executive coaching, have enabled me to write this book for you.

I'll begin by thanking my mom, better known as Coco, for constant inspiration and endless love. I owe her and my entire family a debt of gratitude for countless interactions that served as my first and formative lessons in communication essentials. Likewise, Castle Hills, my childhood home away from home, surrounded me with teachers, youth leaders, and friends who helped me to stay grounded while still growing.

Baylor University is where I discovered the exciting field of communication and met lifelong mentors and friends. I am forever grateful to such wise leaders as Chris Wommack, Dr. Mark Morman, Dr. Eileen Hulme, Dr. Dub Oliver, and Dr. Frank Shushok—all of whom guided me then and inspire me still today. Baylor is also where I formed lifelong friendships with Banes, Fredo, Pete, and Porge. I've managed to make their homes my writing retreats during the production of this book!

I arrived at The University of Texas at Austin for doctoral studies like a sponge and did my very best to soak up every lesson and experience possible. Faculty like Dr. Anita Vangelisti, Dr. Erin Donovan, Dr. Rene Dailey, Dr. Tiffany Whittaker, and Dr. John Daly trained me to think more critically and opened countless doors for me to teach, research, and more. My years at UT-Austin shaped and sharpened me for the journey ahead, and I will be forever grateful to the good people there who afforded me such opportunities.

I was then fortunate to receive a professorship at the University of the Incarnate Word (UIW) in my hometown of San Antonio, Texas, where I am grateful to be part of a learning community that is rich in heritage and mission-driven. UIW is a gem, and having a dean and friend like Dr. Sharon Welkey has made my career all the better! Working with students like Susanna Alford inspires me to give my best every day.

The brief words of gratitude to the aforementioned institutions and people I met within are like glancing at the tree rings of my life. Each ring has been a progressive step in my journey thus far. The friends, family, teachers, mentors, clients, and students I've gained along the way have helped me better understand, teach, and write about the communication essentials.

The actual work of writing and publishing this book introduces a few more essential players. First, I am so grateful to the good people at McGraw Hill. I am inspired by brilliant leaders like Justin Singh who work tirelessly for the good of learners everywhere. I wish every writer the great fortune of working with an editor like Cheryl Segura who has been my perfect dance partner for this project. Cheryl made all my moves look better while simultaneously making all her moves appear effortless. I also owe a debt of gratitude to Ruth Mills who masterfully spotted my weaker writing muscles and showed me how to grow them. Working with Cheryl and Ruth has been a writer's dream.

My secret weapons have been right here at home. My loyal coffee maker desperately deserves a day off. My neighborhood streets endure my daily jogging and give me much needed time and space to ideate. My dear wife, Shannon, is the hero in my story. She loves me unconditionally, sees the very best in me, and cheers me on while I peck away at my keyboard. By now, she has read this manuscript twice as many times as I have, and each time she smiles in awe as if she has stumbled across hidden treasure. It may be years before our kids actually read this book, but their sweet voices and hugs lifted my spirits and found their way to every page. I hope to live my life in such a way that makes Joy, Evy, and Oli proud to call me Dad, because I am over the moon about being their father.

Lastly, I am grateful for you. Let's learn together and continue becoming the best versions of ourselves.

PART I

THE ESSENTIALS

Be a Communication
Student for Life

I'm writing this chapter early on a Tuesday morning, a fact I first learned when the friendly hotel staff gave me a courtesy wake-up call. After placing an order for some coffee and fruit, I do some journaling on my iPad. Next, I listen to my audiobook while knocking out some emails and other urgent messages, followed by Facetiming with my family to wish my kids an enjoyable day at school. Next up, I'm meeting a friend who lives in town for a morning jog and quick bite at his favorite breakfast spot. Then, it's a 90-minute presentation to a group of people I have yet to meet, followed by lunch with the event coordinator, and a series of Ubers and planes to get me home. For now, it's only 6 a.m. Pacific time and I'm still alone in my hotel room, yet communication has and will continue to (ful)fill my day.

Your day may look similar or quite different from mine; however, I am certain that one thing is the same: we both communicate a lot more than we even realize. Some of us have the awareness that we can and should always be improving ourselves as communicators. Whether formally, informally, or without even knowing, we all are students of communication. This is not merely because we receive many inputs of information each day communicated to us in myriad ways. But also, like a snowball rolling downhill, each of us can take our everyday experiences as means for increasing our understanding and abilities as communicative beings.

As a dedicated student of human communication, I strive to do my best at making good sense of the subject, stewarding the discipline, and passing the torch well. Hence, this is not the first book on communication, and it will not be the last. As long as there are communicators who communicate, there will always be more to say about communication. This is partly because of humans' enduring fascination with and connection to the subject matter. Specific topics and titles span from how to find the right words to inspire your team to knowing what to do when there are too many ways to communicate at work. The last three articles I read on communication taught me seven tips for how to nail a hybrid presentation, the delicate art and science of savvy self-promotion, and three strategies for how to ask for help at work without alienating your coworkers. This content wouldn't be produced for a nonexistent audience, so it's clear that there's a real craving for insights that can help us thrive at work and beyond. Though each of us has communicated our entire lives, we are all aware that we can do it better.

We have varying ways of discovering and sharing communication knowledge, skills, and abilities. This book is one such effort. So is coaching a child to be attentive, listen actively, and demonstrate respect when interacting with teachers. So is recommending that a friend wear a blazer and smile more during an interview. Each of us plays a part in the communication learning journey.

And the learning should never stop. That is partly because as much as we evolve as a species, so too do the ways in which we communicate. When I arrived at college in fall 2000, our residence hall had a landline at the front desk that students would use to call home, request a meeting with their professor, or make plans with someone from across campus. Few people owned a mobile phone. Faculty and students were still making sense of this new thing called email, and some were a bit wary of using it. Fast-forward 20 years, and my elementary-aged daughter Facetimed me while writing to ask for my password to download some interactive iPad game that *all* her friends have.

Indeed, communication has been and continues to evolve at lightning speed. And rather than assume innovative technology diminishes old ways of thinking, I find that a return to the fundamentals is necessary for making sense of communication in our modern world. In fact, I find that the communication theories I studied as a doctoral student have become all the more fascinating and informative as the days pass, situations change, and technology disrupts. For this reason, a return to the essentials is, well, essential!

Every chef has essential tools and spices; every artist knows that new colors come from a sophisticated understanding and effective use of primary colors. Likewise, savvy communicators understand that no matter how much things change, you must remain grounded in the communication essentials. This point is one I regularly consider when being contacted for corporate speaking engagements. The requests for communication experts are ever-changing. The top-of-mind issues change, but the foundations of communication don't.

As a recent case in point, in 2020 and 2021 nearly every request I received involved some angle of diversity, equity, inclusion (DEI) and all of them required virtual delivery. Prior to that, the most frequent request was for in-person workshops on topics such as how to communicate like a leader or how to communicate executive presence. What is certain is that any change in the environment or evolution in technology will change the nature of the invitation I receive (e.g., *We really need someone who can help our people figure out how to present effectively using Zoom, Microsoft Teams, or whatever comes next.*). There are countless examples of how an organization may frame its need for an expert to come teach on communicating given the jargon of the day or *en vogue* technology. But no matter the jargon or technology, a large amount of what we must learn stays the same. We have goals as communicators, and we need some help figuring out how to best achieve them.

Whether it's Abraham Lincoln delivering the Gettysburg Address or the guy next to me on the plane snapping a picture of his coffee to tweet about how bad it tastes, *human communication is about people sending and receiving messages to convey meaning and accomplish goals*. Now, trust me, a few scholars in a room could debate ad nauseam over the particulars of the previous sentence, but the general idea will remain. In fact, it can be summed up even tighter: *communication is about messages and meaning*.

THE ROLE OF VISUALS IN COMMUNICATION

The power of visuals in the meaning-making of messages can't be underscored enough. Some visual messages are static while others are dynamic. A stop sign is red and octagon-shaped, and its meaning is indisputable. When you see a stop sign, you must stop. But other symbols are more dynamic, and the associated message may take on a different meaning in a given context. An irate driver extending a middle finger to oncoming traffic is a message with a very different meaning from a college student playfully giving the finger when his best friend beats him at a game of pool.

Visuals also help to emphasize a verbal message. The words "Oh, I just love you" take on a completely different meaning when accompanied by a rolling of the eyes and a sarcastic smirk versus a sincere smile and happy cry. Indeed, there are many nuances and even challenges when constructing the meaning of verbal messages.[1] Without the benefit of context clues or nonverbal behaviors to make the point, we are left to interpret verbal messages as we best understand them. Relying on the words alone can be problematic because much of what we learn about people's thoughts and feelings comes by observing their body language, including watching facial expressions and eye contact.

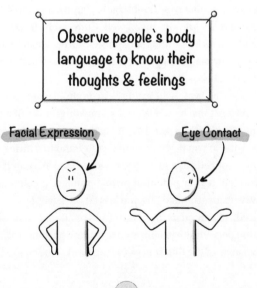

CULTURAL AND RELATIONAL COMMUNICATION

Communication is also cultural and relational. In some families, hugs, kisses, or similar signs of affection are never exchanged, but in others every hello, goodbye, good morning, or good night is reinforced with warm hugs, big smiles, and kisses. The communication norms (to hug or not to hug) within any given family or group can serve to express, and perhaps reinforce, the actual relationships.

When we accommodate our communication style to align with the cultural and relational norms of others, we may be signaling respect and even desire to be part of that group. When we do not accommodate our communication style to the majority group, we may be sending the message that we do not understand, or perhaps, respect the group. If you are a hugger and enter a home insisting on hugging each member of a "nonhugging" family, it is possible they all will oblige and assume you mean well. Conversely, if you are a non-hugger and enter a home and refuse hugs from each member of a hugging family, they may assume that you think yourself better than them and wish to not be associated with any of them.

Imagine if we switch the example to be about whether people engage in a professional handshake when meeting for the first time. Picture yourself with this in mind as you arrive for a job interview. What would it signal to you if you extended your hand to a hiring manager who clearly noticed yet refused your gesture to shake hands? Or, how would you feel if your potential hiring manager greeted you at the interview with an extended hug and kiss on the cheek?

Indeed, all around us the cultural and relational nuances of communication pervade. My clients notice this most when making career moves because of the differences in teamwork, leadership style, and

cultural fit at every company. Given this, new hires should make the time to learn about the people, the company culture, and how individuals interact with one another. New employees tend to pick up the paperwork and processes in their new jobs faster than establishing solid relationships with key stakeholders. Or they discover that it is nearly impossible to be effective at doing their jobs without relating well with the people. Thus, a smart 30-60-90-day onboarding plan will place appropriate emphasis on meeting and cultivating meaningful connection with the right people. Successful professionals understand that achieving high-level priorities and actionable goals is dependent on strong workplace relationships.

FRAMES AND PERSPECTIVES

We've thus far established that communication is symbolic and requires meaning, and that messages and their meanings must be considered in the context of culture and relationships. Additionally, communication involves frames and perspectives. As communicators, we learn to interpret and understand communication in light of the given situation or context—the frame in which the communication occurs. Across the room from me is a painting my wife did last year. It's beautiful and has deep symbolic meaning to our family. It has a nice sturdy frame surrounding it. Both the framed canvas and wall it hangs from are painted, but when a dinner guest points to the wall and asks about the painting, I'm certain he or she is not referring to the white wall. I gather that guest must only be referring to the artwork inside the frame.

Now imagine your life is that wall and holds framed paintings. The framed paintings represent relationships you have and groups you are part of. There may be similarities across the frames, but each is unique. Being attuned to communication frames helps people navigate interactions. For example, when I jog around my neighborhood and my neighbor stops me to ask, "Did you hear that last night?" I know for a fact he is not referring to the big news my sister called to tell me. Nor is he asking about my son who woke up crying in the middle of the night. I know that he is referring to the five seconds of bottle rockets that went off next door to me at around 9:30 p.m. when my very well-meaning neighbors were singing "Happy Birthday" in the driveway. I know this not because I can read his mind, but because it's the only logical frame of reference that this neighbor and I share. And because of that shared frame of reference (i.e., being neighbors who happen to interact from time to time), I'm confident his perspective on the bottle-rocket noise from the night before won't be positive because he's mentioned previously that his pets are sensitive to loud sounds. This frame and perspective help me know how to navigate the conversation quickly so that I can politely exit and continue my run.

Applied in the classroom, I constantly encourage my students to increase their effectiveness when talking with faculty by having them challenge their assumptions and reframe their perceptions. When a student considers the perspective of the faculty member and properly frames how to engage with him or her, that student may increase the likelihood of receiving the extension being asked for. Similarly, by intentionally considering the perspective of your manager and better framing the boundaries and assumptions of interacting with that manager, you may increase the likelihood of receiving extra time off, a desired project extension, the quarterly bonus, or more.

Even if someone understands that communication is about messages and meanings within a cultural context, that person may fail to (re)frame and account for individual perspective. This is a guaranteed way to miss the mark as a communicator, and in some cases may even cause a person to lose a job. Imagine a manager and direct report who traveled together for business. Over the course of travel on Monday, meals and drinks were shared and some personal stories were exchanged. They laughed together for the first time, established a stronger connection, and ended the evening feeling a bit closer. The next morning, they synced-up downstairs in the hotel lobby and headed to the client site. On the ride over, feeling a bit closer to his boss from the day before, the associate jokingly admits being a tad bit hungover. Entering the client site, he gives a fist bump and tells his boss, "Let's do this." At lunch with the client later that day, when referring to his boss, he says, "Trust me, this guy has got some stories to tell."

Fast-forward a few days when they are back at headquarters and the boss calls his direct report in for a quick chat. He shares that next week they'll be traveling separately and he expects a higher level of professionalism from his protégé going forward. This shows just how complex communication can be when it comes to relationships and how people frame their experiences and perspectives. These two did grow closer and friendlier during their travel day. But from the perspective of the manager, the subordinate was not supposed to carry their closeness and friendliness into the frame of workplace interaction.

The key here is to understand that communication is about messages and meanings, which are better understood through cultural and relational context, and we should become adept at applying frames of reference and multiple perspectives when interacting with others and making sense of human interaction.

Communication Constants

These are but a few of the essentials to communication in everyday life that become even more (not less) valuable to us as society evolves and technology disrupts. This is partly because we are members of a global society who are constantly communicating across a variety of mediums. The exact example of the guy traveling with his boss may have just as easily happened 50 years ago before the onslaught of modern technology, but similar communication phenomena described in the story can happen just as easily today while messaging with your boss via smartphone one night and then joining for virtual calls together the next day. This highlights that as we stretch the boundaries of communication in some ways, a savvy communicator will remain grounded in the understanding of the essentials. Like a basketball player preventing traveling, you may spin or otherwise change position with one foot by leaning into a communication venture of your choosing, so long as your pivot foot does not move from its initial position or lose contact with the floor. In our case, that pivot foot must remain planted on the essentials of communication.

ESSENTIAL TAKEAWAYS

At the end of each chapter, you'll find Essential Takeaways. These are the most important points you'll need to carry into your professional and personal lives to find lasting success. In this chapter, the Essential Takeaways are:

- While top-of-mind issues change, the foundations of communication don't.

- Communication is about messages and meaning, and humans communicate to convey meaning and accomplish goals.

- Communication is cultural and relational, and when we accommodate our own communication style to align with the cultural and relational norms of others, we may be signaling respect and even a desire to be part of that group.

Know Why and How
We Communicate

Have you ever really thought about *why* you communicate? For a moment, forget other questions like *when* and *how well* you're communicating and instead focus on the *why*.

All of us have moments when we prefer to be alone, but can you fathom a life of solitude where you couldn't interact with others either face-to-face or virtually? Think of the headlines during the pandemic about sadness, grief, and depression spiking as people tried to adjust to life in isolation and quarantine. Among many other lessons, the pandemic showed us just how much we crave interacting freely with others. Why? Because human communication touches many aspects of our lives, from our individual identity and daily needs to each and every experience with others.

We are inherently social beings. It has long been argued we cannot *not* communicate.[1] We instinctively turn to others for our socio-emotional health, and we suffer physically when denied the ability to interact with others.[2]

Communication helps us to accomplish our personal and professional tasks and goals. Considering even the simplest circumstances, like laundering clothes or getting takeout food, can you imagine accomplishing much of anything without some form of interaction—whether digitally, face-to-face, or a combination of both? Communication is how humans can achieve instrumental needs that may be big (e.g., getting a job or earning a promotion) or small (e.g., ordering a drink or getting called on during a meeting).

Communication helps us maintain our physical and mental well-being and enables us to form and maintain our social and personal relationships. Aside from being born into a family or set up on playdates as a child, the quantity and quality of interactions we have with others is largely a product of if and how we communicate. As early as infants playing peek-a-boo with a parent and toddlers sharing toys on a playground, humans are refining their understanding of how connections with others are associated with the messages communicated verbally and nonverbally.

Communication also helps us understand ourselves—including who we are and who we want to be—by enabling us to share our ideas and express our identities. As a case in point, consider how your attitude and attire may change in the span of any given day, or perhaps even within the hour. Within a month of living together, I could accurately identify the person my college roommate was talking to on the phone just by observing the way he carried himself and by paying attention to the sound of his voice. Many of us have predictable communication behaviors.

What about you? What side of your identity do you show for a job interview? First date? What part of your identity do you perform when gathering with friends on a Friday night? Relatives over a holiday? Consider for a moment how you express these sides of yourself during various occasions, whether in how you dress, the ways you behave, or the things you choose to say or not to say.

ACTIONS, INTERACTIONS, AND TRANSACTIONS

Part of wrestling with why humans communicate requires properly considering the communication process. But even here, scholars have not always agreed. There are three basic models that show how our understanding of communication has evolved over time. The first, the *action model*, suggests that communication is a one-way process. In this view, one person says or does something that sends a message to the other(s). A text message sent that may be read, a voicemail left that may be heard, an outfit worn in hopes of being noticed—these are all examples of communication as action.

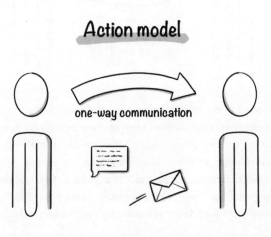

Action model

one-way communication

Going a step further is to see *communication as an interaction*, which implies communication is a two-way street and requires two or more individuals exchanging information. While leaving a voicemail or sending a message is an action, a phone call or rapid exchange of messages captures communication as an interaction. With time, scholars began to see these two models as quite limiting. Communication as an action (e.g., serving a tennis ball) or interaction (e.g., volleying a tennis ball back and forth) fails to explain how rich and dynamic communication can be.

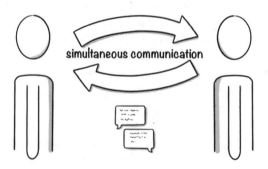

Interaction model

simultaneous communication

This led to the development of a third model, *communication as a transaction*, which seeks to explain how communicators are often sending and receiving messages simultaneously and constructing shared meanings or understandings together.

Rather than seeing these models as good, better, and best, I encourage people to recognize that a given situation will naturally lend itself to be more adequately explained by a particular model.

Transaction model

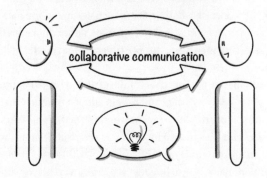

collaborative communication

In order to better understand these different models of communication, let's use an example of a nurse conducting hospital rounds. If a patient says, "Nurse Davis checked my IV and then told me to push the button if I need something," it would suggest that the nurse treated their communication as an *action*. If that same patient says, "Nurse Johnson checked my IV, asked how I was feeling, offered me some water, and then reminded me to push the button if I needed anything," it may suggest that the nurse treated her communication with the patient as an *interaction*. And finally, if the patient reflects on the encounter and says, "Nurse Thompson checked my IV, we discussed my vitals and treatment plan, and then she reminded me to push the button if I need anything," it may suggest the nurse treated their communication as a *transaction*.

The critical difference when it comes to understanding the distinction between an interaction and transaction is that an interaction can simply be exchanging messages without a relational component. Robots can interact. When we interact without a meaningful transaction occurring, we may say something like, "We talked about it, but I don't feel like I was heard or that we reached any sort of understanding." By contrast, when two or more participants create a shared meaning and understanding of information, rather than merely sending and receiving messages, this is a transactional model of communication.

One challenge that even well-informed and well-meaning individuals face is knowing when and how to adopt a transactional model of communication. If a nurse must cover more beds than is reasonably manageable and feels rushed for time, can you really blame him or her for trying to make rounds quickly? Likewise, with so much work to do and information needing to be conveyed in any workplace, we are constantly forced to make decisions about how to communicate.

Imagine you've been invited to interview for an exciting job. The recruiter schedules your interview, but it turns out that you aren't meeting with anyone; instead, you have been given a block of time where you must use a device, connect to a portal, stare at a blank screen, and record your interview answers. There is zero human interaction, much less *transaction*; instead, this is purely an act of regurgitating answers to a blank screen. A mistake people often make is to treat a live interview exactly the same as this one-way act of regurgitating answers to a screen. In the case of a live interview, you would be shortchanging yourself to see an interview as an interaction, where you are asked questions and then reply with answers. A great interviewee knows to be a great conversationalist, who is not just answering questions, but simultaneously reading the interviewer and interacting with that person as if having coffee with a friend. This is the benefit of a transaction model, which helps to account for all the nuance and richness of human communication and which the action and interaction models fail to appreciate.

CHOOSE HOW TO COMMUNICATE

Knowingly and unknowingly, we make many choices when we communicate. Should we speak online or face-to-face? Written or spoken? Dyadic (i.e., between two people), in a group of people, as a public address, or by sending out a mass communication? Regardless of the communication event, essential elements of communication include a source/sender who encodes/creates a message that is sent through a chosen medium to be decoded/received by an audience/receiver. Members of the audience decode the meaning of the message based on their own attitudes and understandings, at which point they may respond to the message verbally or nonverbally. All of this may be subject to competing noise and interference. That is a quick rendition of the textbook explanation. To illustrate the point, let's look at a real-life example.

Imagine that you (the sender) call (phone is your medium) your boyfriend (intended decoder/receiver). After a moment of exchanging the basics of how each other's day has gone, you blurt out, "I can't stand this any longer. I hate not being with you" (message delivered). It makes perfect sense to you to call and say this. After all, you've been dating each other exclusively for six great months but have now spent the past week apart, while your boyfriend visits his family out of state.

The problem is that your boyfriend is watching a movie with his rambunctious nephews when he answers your call on speakerphone. As you speak your heartfelt words, you are competing with children's voices and a movie in the background (noise). He and his nephews heard most of what you said but failed to catch a crucial word. They heard (decoded/received) "I can't stand this any longer. I hate (?) being with you." He didn't hear the crucial word "not" and is now flushed with negative emotion. Confused and slightly embarrassed, he quickly hangs up on you. You glance at your messages to write to him and see what happened, but you notice three dots appear, disappear, and then appear and disappear again. Finally, five minutes later you receive the message, "Are you kidding me right now? I'm done. We can talk tomorrow."

With his phone turned off, you both spend the rest of the night in a state of despair. You are convinced that your bold move to call and express how you feel scared him and led to his whiplash toward breaking up, which you will talk about tomorrow. Meanwhile, he is furious that the person he has been falling in love with waited for him to leave town to call and dump him. Adding fuel to his fire, months ago you two agreed to always manage any conflicts or serious conversations in person because his last romantic partner ended the relationship via text message, a personal experience he found to be traumatizing.

This scenario points to common mishaps in communication. In some form or another, they happen between lovers, siblings, colleagues, and roommates. In this case, the obvious miscommunication culprits include the medium (a phone conversation is less media rich than a video call or face-to-face interaction) and the noise (the boyfriend was distracted by his nephews and the movie they were watching). But, there are other factors worth considering, such as the way the message was crafted and delivered.

We know it's possible to convey our message effectively when communicating by phone and competing against noise. In this case you (the speaker) could have created a clearer message or waited for a quieter moment. Your boyfriend also could have secured a quieter environment for taking the call or asked a clarifying question before assuming the worst and ending the call. We also have to consider the fact that the boyfriend's previous life experiences attuned and heightened his sensitivities to break-up language by phone. Whatever the explanation, just like many communication hiccups, a shared meaning between you two was not achieved. And this shows just how complex communication really is.

Shared meaning is the mutual understanding of a message between sender and receiver. Cocreating a shared meaning is often the goal, and when not achieved, regardless of whether the outcome is positive or negative, a communication failure has transpired. And the impacts can range from inconsequential to lethal. A misunderstood joke between two employees may be shrugged off and forgotten within seconds, or it may lead to a lawsuit. A poorly timed wink and smile from a judge may go unnoticed, or it may inadvertently signal jurors to tilt the scales of justice.

Communicators striving for shared meaning see communication as more than a linear act (like an archer aiming for the bull's-eye) or a back-and-forth exchange (like a game of table tennis). Those seeking shared meaning instead recognize the complex nature of communication, think about context more broadly, and believe that all participants in an interaction are senders and receivers simultaneously. Everyone is part of the messages and meaning-making, including the close-talker, low-talker, no-talker, rambler, eye-roller, arm-crosser, foot-stomper, doodler, eyebrow-raiser, throat-clearer, gum-smacker, and you.

During a presentation, I often look to the audience and ask, "Who is doing the majority of communication right now?" It's a rhetorical question, but still many are inclined to point at me, which is reasonable to think, given that I am the presenter. I proceed by pointing at myself and the crowd simultaneously to make the case that, while I may be sending most of the verbal messages during the presentation, everyone in the room is communicating. Together we are sending and receiving messages to accomplish goals and convey meaning. Those in the audience may be listening to my words and focusing on my non-verbal cues, but I too am absorbing each of the nonverbal cues that I can catch from them. The messages from the audience are a continuous feedback loop informing and compelling me as I nimbly adapt.

In the case of the couple's phone call mentioned earlier, we know that the medium was not media rich (a phone call with distracting noise) and that it's possible the interactants were acting but not transacting, which would explain why the message sent was not the message received and shared meaning was not created. To the degree we understand this essential communication concept, we can better operationalize our knowledge, skills, and abilities for improving ourselves as communicators.

ESSENTIAL TAKEAWAYS

- Human communication touches many aspects of our lives, from our individual identity and daily needs to each and every experience with others.

- Communication helps us to accomplish our personal and professional tasks and goals.

- Communication can be an *action* (i.e., a one-way process), an *interaction* (e.g., a two-way street), or a *transaction* (where communicators construct shared meaning together).

- Communicators striving for shared meaning see communication as more than a linear act (like an archer aiming for the bull's-eye) or a back-and-forth exchange (like a game of table tennis).

Discover the "I" in Communicate

Picture yourself as a water jug. Life experiences and messages fill your jug like water. Your individuality and uniqueness flavors what's in there, like a Kool-Aid pouch. Along the way and throughout your life, a *lot* of messages pour out of your jug.

In working with students and clients over the years, this has been my most helpful way to explain why people communicate so differently. Part of our uniqueness is attributable to the distinct flavor of our Kool-Aid, but then there is also a lot to be said for all those messages and experiences that fill our jug.

FIND THE ROOT CAUSES OF HOW YOU COMMUNICATE

An important reason for pausing on this is because individuals seeking to increase their effectiveness as communicators typically want to jump immediately into evaluating and modifying their communication behaviors without actually exploring the root causes of those behaviors. The reality is that there is a very strong relationship between how people communicate with us, how we see ourselves, and how we then communicate with others.[1] Thus, making outward gains in your communication effectiveness requires doing some *inner work.*

Let me explain further. In most cases, when I have a client who wants help on a big interview for a job, the easiest part of our work together tends to be crafting strong content, while the most challenging part tends to be coaching the client to deliver it well. Why is that the case? Because there's so much to consider when it comes to how each of us experiences the world around us when developing and delivering messages. When coaching, I juggle with questions like: What if my client tends to shut down when sitting across the table from an old white guy? What if my client is triggered every time someone mentions his or her accent? Beyond developing content and rehearsing delivery, imagine the number of outside factors that influence your communication effectiveness. For these reasons, being an exceptional communicator isn't merely learning when to pause; it's also knowing what gives you pause.

Our water jugs are filled by everyday interactions and experiences. But then there are memorable messages that, like it or not, seem to stick with us. For instance, growing up you may have interacted with your primary caregiver nearly every day and perhaps multiple times a day. Certain things your primary caregiver said may echo with you forever, yet not all your interactions are particularly memorable. I don't recall every meal I had with my family as a child, but a handful of things said during certain mealtime conversations left a strong impression on me. On the other hand, I can think of people I dined with only once, yet they said something that stuck with me for years.

The point being, regardless of the person or the nature of your relationship, a memorable message is one that you remember for long periods of time and may potentially influence the course of your life in some meaningful way. I'll never forget when, as a freshman in high school, the principal interrupted my classroom and asked to speak with me in the hall. I was shocked, even a bit nervous, as I walked with him to the corner of the hallway. He proceeded to tell me, "I have a special project . . . I'm asking you to do this because I trust you and I know you will do the right thing." That was more than a quarter century ago. I never forgot that moment nor the words he spoke that day. Years later, I took him to lunch and told him how much it meant to me, all to learn he couldn't recall the moment. There have been handfuls of experiences like that in my life, some positive and uplifting, but others not so much.

These messages can influence the way we see and speak to ourselves; in many cases they become an amplifying loop. To illustrate this, imagine I tell my son that he is a good person and that it makes me proud when he shows kindness to others. I also tell him how much I love his sweet personality and silly sense of humor. He's only two, and it's possible he doesn't fully understand what I am saying to him. But, my hope is that the messages I say to him are taken to heart and he comes to believe them. Ideally, he will grow to internalize and reproduce those words intrapersonally and when communicating with others. Conversely, imagine the words he might begin to internalize and reproduce about himself if he repeatedly heard me tell him that he was a little brat with a horrible personality who would amount to nothing in this world.

Now, let's consider a professional example. My client Kieran is a bright and good-looking guy with a big heart. He is the kind of person you'd trust as your house sitter to water your plants while you were out of town. I could see that when I first met him, but he couldn't. After our first couple of sessions, it was very clear to me that he had some junk in his head that was clouding his ability to see himself for the wonderful person he is. By our third session, I started pushing him to unpack his own thoughts.

He eventually shared with me that he struggled to see himself as worthy of a good job because a decade prior he had been fired from his dream job for misconduct after following a colleague's bad advice. When Kieran's manager learned about the misconduct, he called him in to rant and rave about what a horrible person he was and then terminated him, sending him to his desk with a file-folder box. Years later, Kieran was still hopping jobs, holding his head low, and hoping that his past would never be found out by anyone else, especially future employers. His anxious demeanor and low opinion of himself was most evident when I pressure-tested his behavioral interviewing skills.

The messages we internalize and reproduce about ourselves become a powerful force in shaping our self-identities. In the case of Kieran, when people like me complimented him or said nice things to him, it was like pouring clean water into a muddy water jug. Until we cleaned out those muddy thoughts and self-talk, his own intrapersonal soundtrack was going to taint everything else.

There are numerous tactics for helping people see the fallacy in their negative self-talk and promoting more compassionate intrapersonal messages. For instance, a simple question I ask is, "Would you speak that way about your best friend?" During interview or meeting prep with clients, if I observe that their self-talk is negative, I switch it up on them and we play a game. I ask them the name of their best friend or romantic partner. I then pretend to be a recruiter calling them about this individual, and request they describe the person and list some of the top reasons I should hire them for my company. Magically,

Clean out the bad self-talk!

my clients' lexicon for positive talk is discovered the moment they begin speaking about someone they love. Even more, their nonverbal cues when talking about a friend or loved one are markedly different from when speaking about self.

This was the case with Kieran. When he was able to recognize how easy it was to speak lovely things about others in contrast to how *meh* and *blah* he was when talking about himself, he knew he needed to make some changes. So, we devised plans for how he would spot the patterns in his negative thinking, write them down, create positive reframes for each, and then speak those compassionate words into being. Whenever he was feeling low about himself or ruminating on negative thoughts, he was reminded to be his own best friend at that moment.

People who communicate self-compassion are not ignorant to reality or bad news. Instead, they are striving to think and speak in ways that enhance well-being and professional growth. They communicate honestly, not judgmentally, about failure. They recognize that setbacks and disappointments are a shared human experience. Even though they are keenly aware of their own stumbles, they don't allow themselves to be overtaken with negative emotion.

Kieran has now earned his MBA and is the director of product marketing for a major information technology company. In our time together, we've come a long way in developing his communication skills. Most of our effort, though, started with working on the messages he sends himself.

Time after time, listening to my clients, I see just how much our life experiences and the messages we receive about ourselves continue to influence what we believe about ourselves and the messages we send to others. The same can be said for you and me.

What about you? I hope you would take time to reflect on these questions: What *positive* memorable messages have shaped how you see, think, and speak about yourself? And what negative messages have been hurled at or dumped on you? Are most of these messages from long ago, or are they more recent? What negative messages about yourself should you learn to let go of? What positive messages about yourself should you be clinging to, especially during those challenging times? Questions like these will help you do some of the inner work that helps you to think, feel, and speak better about yourself, which ultimately unlocks greater potential for presenting your best self outwardly.

ARE YOU ON OFFENSE OR DEFENSE?

In working closely with my communication clients, one clear and obvious link I have found is that people who ruminate on negative messages are prone to thinking and communicating defensively. If life were a game of basketball, they would operate like everyone else has the ball and they are merely trying to prevent getting scored on. Conversely, those who ruminate on positive messages are waking each day with a bit more confidence and the optimism of a person who has the ball and is ready to put some points on the board.

By processing the questions just discussed and doing the inner work, you will have a better sense of whether you tend to communicate at work from a place of offense (aka confidence) or defense (aka insecurity). What does that mean exactly? Well, consider this situation. You want to speak with a potential manager about an opening on his or her team. Defensive thinking and messaging may go something like this:

> **Interviewee:** Thanks for making time to talk with me about this opportunity. What can you tell me about the role?
>
> **Hiring Manager:** Well, we are looking to hire the very best. Someone who is going to get in here and crush it.
>
> **Interviewee** (thinking): *Oh, shoot. I'm in over my head and he knows it. He's signaling to me that this was a pity interview. I'm clearly not qualified, and this is embarrassing.*
>
> **Interviewee:** I see. I know it's a stretch for me to have applied for this position, given I don't meet all the qualifications . . . and I am sure that some of your other candidates have more experience than I do . . . but I was encouraged to apply and just go for it.

On the other hand, offensive thinking and messaging may go something like this:

Interviewee: Thanks for making time to talk with me about this opportunity. What can you tell me about the role?

Hiring Manager: Well, we are looking to hire the very best. Someone who is going to get in here and crush it.

Interviewee: That is great to hear because that's precisely why I'm pursuing this opportunity. If I'm fortunate enough to be hired for this role, I assure you I will bring my very best and learn whatever I need in order to get in here and crush it!

Imagine the conversation continues, and the hiring manager asks a basic behavioral-type question. Defensive thinking may go like this:

Hiring Manager: Tell me about a weakness or a time you worked hard to overcome a challenging situation.

Interviewee (thinking): *Oh, wow. I am done. They know I'm unqualified, and they are asking this just to point out that this job is too big for me. They think I'm going to face lots of challenges in this role too. I'm doomed. What was I even thinking when I applied for this role? I feel so stupid.*

Offensive thinking may go like this:

Hiring Manager: Tell me about a weakness or a time you worked hard to overcome a challenging situation.

Interviewee (thinking): *Oh, wow, that's a tricky question, but I got this. I'm going to focus on times that I have successfully overcome challenges! If I have overcome before, I can overcome again in this role, and I need them to know that.*

You can see from these simple examples how our thoughts, which are influenced by the messages we receive, can shape the messages we send about ourselves to others. And the cycle is not necessarily a fair one where privilege plays a major role. That being said, knowing and understanding how certain messages have influenced you and shaped you is important for knowing which you ought to cling to versus dispose of. In our effort to be and communicate the best versions of ourselves, it is important to rid ourselves of negatively influential messages and simultaneously embrace the positive ones. Doing so enables us to begin developing better messages and delivering them with greater impact.

The important question for you now is: How so? How have memorable messages and experiences in your life shaped the way you think about yourself, communicate intrapersonally, and communicate with

Defensive thinking

Offensive thinking

others? Are you prone to communicate from offense (with confidence and positivity) or defense (from a place of insecurity and perhaps even negativity)? How does this change, if at all, given where you are and with whom you are?

ESSENTIAL TAKEAWAYS

- Making outward gains in your communication effectiveness requires doing some *inner work*.

- Messages you've received throughout your life—both good and bad—influence how you communicate with yourself and others.

- Until we recognize and rid ourselves of the negative thoughts about how we communicate, we'll be stuck in a negative loop where we stop ourselves from being the best we can be.

Understand That the Message Sent Is Not Always the Message Received

It was my first day as a freshman in college. I had arrived to class early, determined to take a seat in the front row. Having never been known as top of the class, sitting in the front row seemed like my best chance of making a positive first impression on my professors starting day one. You may know an unspoken expectation is that the first day of a college class is usually just "syllabus day," when the professor engages with the students a bit, shares a few expectations for the course, and passes out the syllabus, all before ending class early and sending people on their merry way.

This, however, was not the case for this class. Our professor decided to begin lecturing from course materials on day one. After about 30 minutes passed, I looked around the room and saw that most of my peers were distracted or falling asleep. Determined to start the semester strong and make a good impression, I fought the urge to get distracted and paid very close attention.

Bright-eyed and ready for anything, I sat enthralled as the professor spoke words to me that I have never forgotten. Now, technically, it wasn't said *only* to me. There were a couple hundred of us in the room. But the words he said hit me so deeply that it felt like he had shared a secret with only *me*. And I have shared this secret with thousands of people ever since: "Nay, nay, nay. The message sent is not always the message received." I looked around the room to see if anyone else was awakened by this monumental declaration. To my surprise, everyone was perfectly still as if nothing had happened. How could this be? The good professor had just said a mouthful. *The message sent is not always the message received!* I am sure that I already knew this. But throughout the day I kept repeating the sentence to myself, thinking about seemingly complicated situations that I could explain away by applying this uncomplicated statement.

WHAT HAPPENS WHEN MESSAGES ARE MISUNDERSTOOD

Sure, anyone could tell you about a simple misunderstanding or misinterpretation, but my mind was entranced with questions like: What exactly happens when the message sent is not the message received? Just how far does this problem manifest itself? How much damage is done at the hands of (mis)communication?

These thoughts stayed with me all semester, and I began to recount situations a bit differently. I asked my peers if they could think of examples when the message sent was not the one received. One guy down the hall told us over dinner about how much trouble he got in when he missed curfew by 12 hours. Allegedly, he took his parents' demand of "Be home before 11" to mean, "Be home in the morning in time for church." It was funny when he told us, but I am certain it wasn't funny at the time.

The idea that the message sent is not always the message received is all around us. Fans of the TV show *Friends* can tell you that Ross and Rachel clearly did not see eye to eye on what it meant for their relationship to be "on a break." In fact, most of our popular programming is riddled with messages sent but not received.

From Main Street to Wall Street. From your house to the White House. The problem of the message sent not always being the message received is everywhere—and it can be quite consequential. But how big of a concern should this be for us?

DO YOU KNOW WHAT YOU'RE COMMUNICATING?

Well, think about yourself as a communicator. When and how are you communicating? The answer to when is simple: from the moment you wake, you are communicating. It's not just the words you speak either. It is the messages you type, the way you move and gesture, and even how you dress and accessorize yourself.

Pause right now. Assess your attire, your posture, the look on your face. Without even murmuring a word, what information would someone gather about you if that person had one glance at you? What opinions would the person form of you? In what ways would those opinions be shaped by what you are doing? In what ways might those opinions alter based on who the observer is and what biases that person carries?

What message are you sending across?

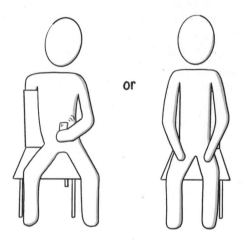

or

That is just one freeze-frame in time. Now multiply that by every moment in your day and add the actual words you speak and how you say them, plus the messages you type and send across platforms and devices. Suffice it to say, we are constantly sending and receiving messages, some intended and others not.

We are communicative beings. While we may not always be on a stage delivering a formal address to a large audience, we are regularly presenting ourselves, as well as making sense of others' messages and behaviors.

Jane Brody with the *New York Times* said it this way:

> The importance of accuracy in communication is underscored by the fact that we send and receive nonverbal messages virtually all our waking hours when we are with

other people. Though we may say nothing with words, our facial expressions, gestures, posture, body position and manner of dress continually send very telling messages. When we speak, our tone, velocity and volume of speech convey additional meaning.[1]

If we are constantly communicating, then we are regularly sending messages that may not actually be received as we intended. And we may regularly receive messages not as they were intended. Now, some may be quick to say, "OK, I get it. We communicate all the time. But the truth is I am a great communicator. I know plenty of people who should work on their communication skills and could use this book. But I'm good." The truth is that our effectiveness as communicators matters. And the problem is that most people are not as effective as they think they are or wish that they could be!

ESSENTIAL TAKEAWAYS

- The message sent is not always the message received.
- From the moment you wake, you are communicating—not only with the words you speak but also in the messages you type, the way you move and gesture, and even how you dress and accessorize yourself.
- Think about what information someone would gather about you if he or she had one glance at you. What opinions would the person form of you?

CHAPTER

5

Commit to Being Effective

I am not a perfect communicator. Nor am I the world's greatest dad.

Don't get me wrong, I am a loving and devoted father, but just because my younger daughter smiles and calls me the world's greatest dad every time I bring home her favorite pizza doesn't make it true. She certainly doesn't call me the world's greatest dad each time I remind her to make her bed or pick up after herself. But if I only tallied the times I brought home pizza, I could falsely presume that the greatest dad title is mine.

The same can be true for how we rank ourselves as communicators. When sharing your big idea to a room of fellow supporters, don't count the nodding heads and call them converts. Your staunch supporters nodding their heads have not been converted to your viewpoint, they are merely reinforcing a mutually shared view or trying to encourage you as a friend.

Nods from your supporters don't make you the world's greatest communicator any more than buying pizza makes me the world's greatest dad. A better indicator of your effectiveness as a communicator would be to take your passionate plea to a room of nonsupporters or neutral individuals and then count those who bought your message. Those are your potential converts.

LISTEN TO ALL THE FEEDBACK YOU RECEIVE

This is an important concept to wrestle with because, while some people may have a negative and unassured view of self when it comes to their effectiveness as a communicator (e.g., "I'm no good, let someone else say it"), there are those who have a self-serving, perhaps overly confident, view of their effectiveness as a communicator (e.g., "I'm the best, people love me, let me own the message").

I see this firsthand as a communication instructor and coach. People will point to the indicators suggesting they are doing quite all right as a communicator but then come to me confused by a negative performance review. One client experienced this and said, "I really don't get it. This review makes me out to be a monster who yells all the time, but my direct reports think I am hilarious. They always laugh at my jokes." This client is not alone in wanting to reject negative feedback. Most of us want to defend ourselves when we first receive critical feedback. Having an open mind to a challenging idea (such as a performance review that indicates areas where we might need to grow) is much harder than finding all of the reasons we're perfectly fine the way we are. (Comments like "The people I supervise seem to like me" do exactly that.) Change is hard, and so is admitting that you aren't perfect as is. But the reality is you're doing yourself a disservice when you dismiss feedback you don't like and only focus on what you want to hear instead.

This phenomenon goes beyond work and home. I am reminded of a recent outing I made to get my hair cut. Between teaching classes, I slipped over to the nearby barbershop for a quick trim. I was there only 10 minutes and was out $10, but I got so much more than I paid for. The loud and lively fellow in the chair next to me was ranting and raving about his wife. He carried on for five minutes about how she is always nagging him to put his phone down, smile more, and pay more attention to the family. The patient hairdresser listened intently, nodding her head and showing empathetic eyes and facial movements as she continued to cut his hair.

This conversation was hard enough to overhear, but the last line he said as he left said it all: "See, now why can't my wife be more like you? You actually get me!" My jaw dropped. To be clear, this man was not hitting on his hairdresser. Instead, he was revealing his unwillingness to receive negative feedback from someone who should matter most (his spouse) and an instinctual need to receive acceptance and approval, even if it required the cost of a haircut.

For my client who received a negative review for outbursts in meetings, it's a lousy retort to proclaim, "But the interns think I am funny!" And for the guy in the barbershop whose wife wants him to put his phone down and smile more, it would be ridiculous to stand on the argument, "But my hairdresser understands me!"

UNDERSTAND THE MOTIVES OF YOUR AUDIENCE

We communicate in a world riddled with power dynamics, and thus we must be wise to how our positions of power influence our interactions with others. We must also make note of how power dynamics may hinder our ability to receive accurate feedback on our effectiveness as communicators. Power dynamics are always a factor in communication. Employees smiling during a staff meeting but secretly disliking their boss is akin to college students pretending to laugh at the professor's jokes but secretly just wanting to make a good impression in hopes of earning an A, which is not much different than the hairdresser politely affirming the rants of her patron in expectation of a generous tip. Each of these examples is a reminder for us to never forget the role that power dynamics play in our communication with others.

In your journey to becoming a more effective communicator, regularly take inventory of your interactions and consider how power impacts people's thoughts, feelings, and behaviors. Start with this question: Why does interviewing someone feel so different than being interviewed by someone? With everything else staying the same, the only actual difference is that one person is guiding the conversation with a set of questions. So why does it feel so different?

Next, think about questions like these: Are you as confident and capable of a communicator when having a one-on-one with your manager as you are when having a one-on-one with a peer or perhaps someone you manage? If those interactions look and feel different, take a moment to reflect on how so and why that might be. When presenting to audiences, are you as able to captivate the attention of those who don't report to you, agree with your thinking, or owe you anything? How effective are you at making friends and forming alliances with people who don't look like you or share similar worldviews?

For those who find themselves spending more and more time on the stage, it's important to regularly reflect on what it feels like to sit in the audience. Likewise, for those who have achieved positions of authority, it is important to regularly reflect on what workplace interactions felt like before stewarding such power. To be a truly effective communicator, you need reliable feedback loops and must consider not only the perspective, but also the position, of all participating parties. This becomes increasingly important as your career elevates.

EFFECTIVE COMMUNICATORS CONSIDER THEIR INTENT *AND* THEIR IMPACT

One benefit of reliable feedback loops is that you will have a mechanism for knowing how the messages you send are being received. Another way to think of this is that feedback loops help you understand the impact of your messages and the meanings they convey. An important skill for communicators is learning how and when to own not only the intent of their messages but also their impact on others. I strive to keep ample feedback loops in my life, knowing that I need honest input from numerous sources on a number of things to keep me aware of when my intentions are not aligning with my impact.

I had a rather humorous experience with this a couple of summers ago while at the pool with my family. We were splashing around and having fun when a friend offered to snap a picture of all of us. It turned out great, and because we rarely get a good picture altogether, I proudly posted it on social media right then and there.

While swimming, I received some "likes" and flattering comments. It felt affirming to see that people responded favorably to the picture of my cute family. A while later, while still at the pool, one of my best friends called and said, "Dang, dude, were you just itching to show off those biceps? Nice!" He was being playful and teasing me. It was funny, and he did make me laugh.

But after we hung up, I thought about his comment a little longer. My *intent* for posting the photo was instigated by being overjoyed at having a flattering picture with my family at the pool and then wanting to share it on social media. But my friend's comment revealed what probably many people had *assumed* about my intentions but would never say: "OK, we get it. You work out and want the world to know." It mortified me to know that the message intended might not have been the one received.

I strongly considered deleting the photo, and here is why: I believe effective communicators take responsibility not only for the intentions behind their messages, but (within reason) also the impact of their messages. If the impact of posting the photo would reasonably cause people to assume that the intentions were negative, selfish, or attention-seeking, then I'd rather take down the photo than have anyone think about it for another second. In other words, I can't only be interested in the intentions behind my messages. I must remain invested in the impact my messages have on the recipient(s). If the message I'm sending is not the one received, that concerns me because it will affect my audience and, ultimately, me and my goals as a communicator.

In the end, I decided to leave the photo up because I knew it would make a great story to tell my class. And I was right. It's become an excellent, self-deprecating example of intent versus impact and how the message sent is not always the message received.

On numerous occasions, clients have commented to me that they would rather not concern themselves with the impact of their messages, thinking that their only job is to know their material, communicate accurately, and leave it for others to catch up or figure it out. For a number of reasons, this just doesn't work. Namely, as a communicator, you have goals, and it is only through your audience that you achieve these goals. Thus, you must be highly invested in how you are received and the impact your communication has on others. This requires you to be receptive to feedback and open to grow.

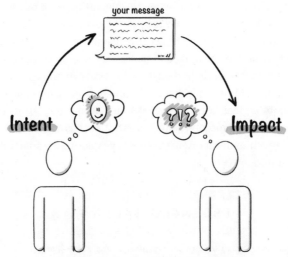

Remember: the message sent is not always the message received

ALWAYS BE OPEN TO GROW

Whether it be a text message that went awry, the social media post that my friends tease me about, or any number of experiences, I allow these instances to sharpen me as a communicator. I approach public speaking the same. If someone doesn't laugh at something I thought was funny, there must be a reason. Rather than chalk it up as an audience problem, I need to consider ways to modify my messages and deliver them better to enhance my communication effectiveness.

If we want to grow in our effectiveness as communicators, we can't get bent out of shape when people misinterpret or dislike the messages we are sending. We must rise above and be willing to learn and adapt. Communication is central to our lives. And our successes in life are undeniably linked to the effective use of communication skills. Given this, it is important to understand communication essentials and be able to apply them well. Understanding the contents of a cookbook is great. Learning to cook well is even better. So, how do we go about communicating better? In Part II, we take a close look at enhancing communication effectiveness by exploring the points of a star communicator.

ESSENTIAL TAKEAWAYS

- You're doing yourself a disservice when you dismiss feedback you don't like and only focus on what you want to hear instead.

- If we want to grow in our effectiveness as communicators, we can't get bent out of shape when people misinterpret or dislike the messages we are sending. We must rise above and be willing to learn and grow.

PART II

THE ESSENTIALS APPLIED

Communication Self-Assessment

Now that you *understand* the essentials, you're ready to *apply* the essentials. To get started, complete the benchmark assessment below. Your answers will help to highlight the areas you can target in Part II to make the most dramatic improvement in your communication skills. No one else needs to see this, so feel free to be brutally honest.

Directions: Please read each statement and use the following scale to indicate how strongly you agree with it. Then add up the rating column for a total score at the bottom.

    1 = Never
    2 = Rarely
    3 = Sometimes
    4 = Usually
    5 = Always

Rating	
	I communicate in ways that help me to accomplish my personal and professional goals.
	I have the desire and willingness to improve my communication skills so that I accomplish more of my goals.
	I know how and when to accommodate my communication style to align with the cultural and relational norms of those around me.

	I establish a clear understanding of my goals and audience before developing content that will be sent or delivered.
	I communicate in ways that prioritize my big-picture goals over my immediate interests and short-term needs.
	I can pinpoint negative thoughts and manage them before they compromise my ability to communicate effectively.
	I choose "offense/positive" messaging and confidence over "defense/negative" messaging and insecurity.
	I demonstrate active listening skills and limit distractions when meeting and interacting with others.
	I am intentional with the nonverbal messages I send (e.g., clothes I wear, eye contact, posture, facial cues, and gestures).
	I communicate with clarity, and keep my messages simple, rather than complicate them.
	I communicate concisely and focus my messages on what others must know, not merely on what I want to say.
	I make my messages engaging and captivate people with storytelling.
	I project confidence with my visual delivery skills (e.g., eye contact, posture, and gesturing).

	I sound confident when I speak (e.g., project well, use minimal filler words, and pause effectively).
	I select the best communication medium (e.g., messaging, phone call, virtual meeting, or in-person) according to my goals and audience.
	I structure my oral and written messages to have logical flow.
	I make positive first impressions when meeting new people and know how to build upon those positive impressions in future interactions.
	I am adept at making and maintaining social and professional relationships.
	I communicate effectively through conflict and difficult conversations.
	I am a gracious communicator who believes that everyone is capable of enhancing their communication effectiveness.
	Maximum Score: 100

Add up your total score to determine your percentage of the 100 possible points. This score is only the "starting line"—a way to help measure your progress as you learn more about communication applications in this Part, "The Essentials Applied." Once you've had a chance to practice new communication strategies, you can repeat this assessment to track your growth.

Right now, this benchmark assessment can also help you gain some valuable insights into your specific communication skill levels. Any statements that you ranked as 4 or 5 may represent your strengths as a communicator. Statements that you ranked as 1, 2, or 3 provide you with opportunities for improvement.

Circle or highlight the three to five statements where you indicated the lowest scores. As you work through Part II and begin to practice some of your communication skills in real time, pay close attention to those areas. If you focus on accelerating those particular skills, you'll likely see the biggest change in your communication performance and results.

Your Communication Starting Point: Be Willing

Part I introduced essential communication concepts through the lens of everyday life, but especially workplace interactions. Knowing these essential concepts is critical but still only half the battle. To actually master the communication essentials requires putting them into action. In this second part, we apply a practical framework—being a star communicator—which will equip you with five simple but crucial elements of communication that will help you reimagine each professional encounter as an opportunity to shine brighter.

In some form or another, your job requires you to present. It may not be on a stage. It may not even be in person. But in some way, your workplace interactions have a presentational component. While most people may not realize this, presenting is something that all of us do nearly every day. Whether it's fielding client questions on a virtual call, defending a position to your manager and team, delivering a demonstration or actual presentation, or just speaking to an audience of one during a job interview, you are regularly presenting in the workplace. And for some people, these presentational moments can be terrifying. Some people avoid them at all costs. When describing the dreaded presentational act of public speaking, actor and comedian Jerry Seinfeld joked:

> I saw a study that said the number one fear of the average person is public speaking. Number two is death. Death is number two! How in the world is that? That means to most people, if you have to go to a funeral, you would rather be in the casket than doing the eulogy.[1]

While few jobs require formal public speaking, the reality is you don't have to be on a stage to feel the presentation anxiety that Seinfeld is referencing. Most people I know stress over writing memos, dread giving updates in meetings (especially when leaders are present), have major anxiety about interviewing, and generally prefer to minimize or avoid interactions where it feels like a spotlight has been placed over their heads. Maybe you can relate to my clients who say, "I'm not sure what would be worse: to stay in this job or go through the painful experience of interviewing for another job." There may be plenty of things about interviewing that people find unpleasant, but for most people, it's having to prepare and present yourself to a person or people you know are evaluating you.

So before diving into a framework designed to help you communicate more effectively, it is important to pause and recognize that applying it at all will require a critical first step—*willingness*.

Workplace interactions create endless opportunities to present yourself and communicate your ideas. Some people shy from them, others shine in them. Just like the hardest part of any morning jog is choosing to get out of bed and lace your shoes, for some the decision to be a more willing communicator is a monumental first step.

To know and effectively apply the communication essentials is life-elevating. To be unwilling is to rob yourself of an incredible gift. As a small comparison, the iPad completely elevated my graduate school experience, and I've used one ever since. As an early adopter, I have also gifted the iPad to family members and close friends on occasion in hopes that they too will benefit from the magic of the device. Sometimes this works out as hoped and they utilize the product to its full potential. But sometimes, they thank me, look at it for a bit, and then leave it on a shelf to collect dust. Sure, I can send them tips, tricks, and how-to videos on how to unlock the potential of such a powerful machine, but for what? Until the other person decides he or she is *willing* to embrace and maximize the potential of the new iPad, my efforts will be wasted. For the record, I am not trying to sell you an iPad. Instead, I am telling you that applying the communication essentials can be life-changing and career-altering, but you'll never know unless you try.

As someone who teaches other people about how to enhance their communication abilities, I have learned that before teaching anyone *how to do* something, that person must first demonstrate a desire and willingness to actually *want to do* the work to improve. Like a new device or even a gym membership, the tools for effective communication are only beneficial if you actually choose to use them.

IT'S ALL ABOUT MINDSET

There may be many reasons why people would be unwilling to put themselves out there and be the message bearer. For many, the explanation has to do with mindset. Most of what we understand regarding mindset is often credited to Carol Dweck, renowned Stanford psychologist. Her research highlights how individuals with a fixed mindset believe their basic abilities and talents are deep-seated and unchangeable. These people believe they are incapable of improving or developing, whereas those with a growth mindset understand their talents and abilities can be developed through effort, learning the right things, and persistence.[2]

Consider what it means to be "a math person." Evidence of a fixed mindset is revealed each time we say or hear phrases like "I'm not much of a math person." As a young person, I was utterly convinced that I was not a math person. Most of my teachers perpetuated this very myth. By sixth grade, I learned what to do when I saw a challenging math problem. I either guessed the answer, turned to a math person for the answer, or scratched my head and looked confused just long enough for a teacher to come and help.

Later in life, I learned the truth of what makes a math person: the person does the math problems. When these people get stuck, they consult the book, ask for clarification, and give the question a little more time. Ultimately, they work through it and figure out math problems one at a time, which gives them the knowledge and skills to tackle the next set of problems. Their growth mindset is the reason they stick with it and do the math, thereby becoming a math person.

Our mindset is powerful. Individuals who believe they are not a math person are not going to even try to solve the math problem. The person who claims to not be a runner and refuses to lace up has no hope of running a 5k. Similarly, step one in growing as a communicator is adopting a growth mindset and demonstrating a willingness to try.

Many of my clients suggest that they don't demonstrate a willingness to communicate because the novelty of speaking up intimidates them or the fear of evaluation is too great. Whether the reason is novelty, fear of being evaluated, or something else, the reality is that all of us experience physiological arousal when facing certain communication events. You experience physiological arousal when your heart starts racing, butterflies take over your stomach, your palms get sweaty, and more.

There are smart ways to work through communication anxiety. A lot of really interesting research has looked at how people experience similar types of physiological arousal from events like riding a roller coaster and speaking in public. In the instance of riding a roller coaster or giving a presentation, all of us experience physiological arousal *but* we don't all think of it the same way. The physiological changes lead some to say, "I am so excited, my heart is racing, and I can't wait to take a turn on that roller coaster." While others say, "I am so scared, my heart is racing, and I better sit this one out and just watch others ride."

For example, I have one client whose neck turned bright red every time she sensed she was about to be called on in a meeting. She was so determined to grow as a communicator that, despite the physiological arousal she was experiencing, she started asking to be put on the meeting agenda, and she began wearing scarves to meetings to prevent others from noticing her anxiety. We polished her talking points, rehearsed them the day before, and within a month, she felt the success of not only communicating effectively in weekly meetings but also overcoming her anxiety.

After experiencing success as a communicator, she has reprogrammed herself to welcome the adrenaline she gets as something exciting, rather than something to fear. Needless to say, she doesn't need the scarves anymore.

So the trick to overcoming a fear of communicating is not to get rid of physiological arousal, but instead to recognize it as normal. If a racing

heart and a stomach full of butterflies is your reality, then the questions are: How will you make sense of it when it happens? Will you be someone who assumes that the presence of physiological arousal is reason to pass the microphone and hide? Or will you be someone who harnesses the physiological arousal as the fuel you need to shine as a star communicator?

I see in my clients that a little willingness can be the spark that lights a fire within. When you see that your willingness is appreciated, allow your positive feedback from others grow your confidence, which can also breed even greater willingness. It's an amplifying loop wherein willingness produces more willingness. So, whether it be a call for a volunteer to send out meeting notes, make a proposal to decision makers, or give a wedding toast, raise your hand and go for it.

GETTING STARTED WITH EFFECTIVE COMMUNICATION

Before we dive into how to enhance our communication effectiveness, take a second to pause and consider what you believe makes for effective or ineffective communication. Think back to memos, meetings, hard conversations, and presentations where people have impressed you the most. Which individuals come to mind when considering great communicators? What were they doing that made them so effective? Conversely, consider situations where communicators were less than impressive. What were they doing (or not doing) that made them ineffective? And, finally think about yourself. In what situations have you felt most effective or ineffective as a communicator?

When thinking through questions like these, most people I work with tend to answer quite similarly. Most of us appreciate when people speak and write clearly, demonstrate confidence, inspire us to action, and listen well. There is also a common belief that intentionality and preparation are key to communicating better.

But not all preparation is of the same quality. Some activities may cause you to feel prepared, but they really only burn time. Sitting at your desk and searching the web for that perfect graphic or video is not the smartest way to prepare for a meeting, but it does burn time and can even make you feel like you are "preparing." Memorizing your résumé and reciting your accomplishments into a mirror takes time, but it is not the best way to prepare for a job interview. In Part III, we take a deep dive into the smartest ways for you to prepare for interviews and more.

A central purpose of this book is to equip you with the communication essentials that lead to greater success in the workplace, but equally important is to ensure that these essentials are memorable and simple to apply. Your day job is challenging enough; this book should make your life easier, not harder.

When it comes to enhancing our communication, it is possible to be intentional and keep it simple. The framework I share with you now highlights that the fundamentals of communicating effectively come down to five core elements, which are easiest to visualize on a star.

This star captures the best of what we know for how to communicate effectively, and it is what my students and clients have learned to reference before taking a call, clicking send, or presenting. It is what I have taught to CEOs, university presidents, professional athletes, college students, my own children, and thousands of others. It could be complicated in a variety of ways, but why would we do that? The sparkle and shine of it, instead, is in the simplicity.

A STAR HAS FIVE POINTS

Every act of communication begins with a *goal*. Attainment of the goal depends on *audience perception* of the *messenger* and their *message* in a given *medium* (e.g., email, phone call, face-to-face interaction, live performance, text, video, audio recording, etc.). These are the five points: goal, audience perception, messenger, message, and medium.

Let's try an example.

Imagine you want to persuade your friends or coworkers to eat sushi tonight (goal), and you are considering how they might think, feel, and respond (audience perception) to you (messenger) if you send a sushi and a heart emoji (message) to your group chat (medium).

Each of these variables may influence goal attainment. If your friends have been ghosting on the group chat, then you likely picked

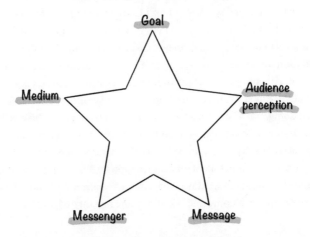

Communication Star

Goal

Medium

Audience perception

Messenger

Message

the wrong *medium* for communicating. If your friends misinterpret the sushi and heart emoji and think you are saying, "I just ate sushi and wow I love it," then the subtlety of your *message* may ultimately lead to a failure on your part. If you have a reputation with your friends for picking great restaurants, then your credibility as a *messenger* will work in your favor. If not, and your reputation for picking restaurants is suspect, then you are better off trying another tactic.

Some readers may wonder about additional variables, such as the *timing of a message*, which is critically important to goal attainment. The truth is that *time* is a critical factor that plays into each of these variables. Case in point: if one of your friends threw up from eating sushi yesterday, then this will impact *audience perception* (at least with the one who got sick) and compromise your ability to achieve your *goal*.

Now let's walk through how this framework applies to a workplace scenario. Imagine you have been asked to give a presentation in the next couple of days. This is part of a three-hour meeting that happens each month and includes your manager's manager (aka your skip-level manager). Your manager asked you to give a 20-minute presentation on an initiative that you and your team have been working on. When it comes to whether your audience is warm to you and your initiative, you know that your manager is in favor of the work you've been doing, but that *her* manager is unsure if the cost will be worth it. You also know that you aren't the only one presenting an initiative on the call and each presenter is vying for the same resources.

You can organize all of this information by filling out a Five Points of the Communication Star chart, which I recommend you do each time you are developing and delivering any message of consequence.

Five Points of the Communication Star

Goal (Professional or Personal)	Audience Perception	Message (Content)	Messenger (You)	Medium (The Details)
Want people to say: "This is outstanding work! We will proudly support your new initiative."	My manager is supportive. Don't know what my manager's manager thinks yet.		18 months in role No negative interactions with those attending	This is a two-hour virtual meeting happening next Tuesday morning.

or "Wow! This person seems capable and ready for next-level work. He (or she) is on deck for promotion!"	Peers will be in meeting, also presenting, and are competing for same resources. Who else will be attending?		Have had very little exposure to my manager's manager Some of my peers still "little brother" me Earned "excellent" but not "role-defining" on last performance evaluation	My proposal happens at the start of the second hour, after 10-minute break. It's a corporate deck; I can insert five slides max; amending the deck is not allowed. Most are working remote, but it might look nice if I presented from office at work.

My clients find this chart to be beneficial professionally and personally. What you will notice in the example is that "Message" is the last section to be completed, and this is because, even while you might have general ideas about what you may say, producing your actual message content will require deep analysis of other critical variables, such as goal and audience. I advise you (like I advise my clients) to establish a clear understanding of your goal, audience, how your audience likely perceives you, and communication medium, *before* crafting your message.

The next time you are responsible for sending out a memo or providing an update in a meeting, try filling out this chart. You likely have some initial goals that you can jot down, but chances are you will refine your goals as you process through the next series of questions. So you can start by describing your *audience*:

- Who are the intended recipients?

- What is in this for them?

- Are they eager to receive your message?

- Are they dreading your message?

- Do they supervise you?

- Do they report to you?

How does this audience see you, the *messenger*?

- Do they have high expectations of you and see you as a high-potential person?

- Are they considering your promotion next month?

- Do they not even know you yet?

Next, describe the *medium*:

- Is it five minutes in an all-hands meeting?

- How long is the entire meeting?

- Are you at the beginning, middle, or end of the meeting?

Now that you have answered some basic questions about your audience, the likely perception of the messenger (i.e., you), and your medium, you may wish to refine your initial goals. I encourage you to think of your actual goals as sound bites for what you wish the audience would say about you and your message after receiving it.

The first few times you go through this process, you may realize that the more clearly you refine one variable, the more motivated you are to tweak another. For instance, better clarity around the people in your audience and how they perceive the messenger (you) is likely to expand your thinking around your goal. Each of the remaining chapters in Part II focuses on uncovering and applying one of the five different points of the star (goal, audience, message, messenger, medium). Learning to effectively apply these five points is how you master the communication essentials.

ESSENTIAL TAKEAWAYS

- The first step to communicating more effectively needs to be your willingness to speak in front of others.

- Like a new device or even a gym membership, the tools for effective communication are only beneficial if you choose to use them.

- A star communicator focuses on five points: the goal, the audience's perception (of the messenger), the message, the messenger, and the medium.

- Establish a clear understanding of your goal, your audience, how your audience likely perceives you, and your communication medium, *before* you craft your message.

CHAPTER 7

Identify Your GOAL

Communication Star

Goal

Medium

Audience perception

Messenger

Message

You have the potential to shine as a star communicator. Your first objective is to define your communication goal because why would you even be communicating if you didn't have a goal? Like a voyager without a compass or map, a communicator without a goal is lost and merely stumbling through the unknown. It can be easy to communicate on autopilot, causing you to either forget your goals or fail to achieve them. This is especially true in the workplace, where people tend to be strapped for time and are desperately trying to wade through so much noise and information being communicated at them.

We have a way of sensing when someone doesn't have a goal or is failing to achieve it. Halfway through a meeting or presentation, or when reading an email or memo, have you ever thought something like:

I don't get it. What is the point?

What are they even saying right now?

What is this email even about?

I don't understand why this is my issue.

Why exactly did you stop by to see me?

Am I supposed to do something with all of this?

Chances are you think these thoughts more than you realize. And, while it's sad to say (and maybe hard to hear), chances are someone has thought these things of you, too. Having these thoughts is not necessarily rude. Nor does it imply that someone is being lazy or incapable of understanding. As individuals whose brains are programmed to make sense of things, we merely want to understand the world around us. Additionally, humans tend to believe their lives are massively important, and, therefore, they hate to think their time is wasted.

So within the first sentence or two of an email or in the first minutes of a conversation, we want to solve the riddle: *What is the message here, and why does it matter to me?* This isn't just a mindset of the stressed-out executive. All of us are trying to make sense of the messages around us and the individuals conveying them—it's part of our ingrained survival techniques.

This is why, before you ever start drafting your message or playing in a slide deck, you must get very clear about your goal. What do you want others to think, feel, believe? How do you want them to be-have? This doesn't necessarily make you a greedy or selfish person, ei-ther. While some goals may be self-serving, others can be incredibly thoughtful, even altruistic. Likewise, there are times when it is advan-tageous to declare your goal (e.g., "I want you all to support this plan"). Then, there are some goals that are better achieved when kept to your-self (e.g., "I want people to respect me"). Your goals for any particular communication can be any number of things, such as, *I am [writing you, calling you, speaking to you] today to*:

- *Raise money*

- *Win a vote*

- *Persuade a room*

- *Be liked*

- *Gain respect, show respect*

- *Show leadership*

- *Convey information, learn information*

- *Gain a friend, grow my network*

- *Demonstrate care*

- *Recruit volunteers*

- *Convince colleagues to meet me for lunch at my favorite café*

Whether you have come to recognize it or not, each workplace communication can be purposeful and achieve goals. The sooner you determine your communication goals, the more intentionally you can move toward them, and the more likely you are to achieve them.

RETHINKING COMMUNICATION GOALS

Picture the last meeting you had with an influential leader in your organization, or picture the last time you interviewed for a job. If you had any advance notice, you likely chose to wear a nice outfit with the intent of wanting to impress someone. It may not seem like it, but that is a goal. Sometimes we stand before a room of people to encourage them to vote in a way that we wish they would. Sometimes we send a note to someone for the sole purpose of keeping the connection warm. These are all goals. Whatever your goal, know it and own it.

There is a simple exercise for identifying your communication goal, and I encourage you to try it. The next time you have an important conversation or plan to send an important note, be sure that you can complete the following: *The purpose of my communication is to_____*. Until you can fill in the blank, don't start thinking about or typing the content of your message. You can't have clear messaging until you have a clear goal.

I recently had a client who was flying from Chicago to San Francisco for an important meeting. To prepare for the meeting, I had him draft his goals, and then we refined them together. In the end, we came up with three:

The purpose of this meeting is to (1) persuade my clients that I fully understand their problem and am capable of solving it for them; (2) persuade my clients that the solution I am providing will meet their needs and even exceed their expectations; and (3) instill in my clients the confidence that I am a trustworthy and likable partner that they would prefer to work with today and in the future.

It's important to point something out about my client's meeting. He had more than one goal, and you can too. Regardless of the number of goals, all your preparation and development should be centered and focused on accomplishing them. As you draft and prepare, continue asking yourself, *How does this help me accomplish my stated goal(s)?* Anything not advancing your goal is potentially betraying it. To have a communication goal is like eyeing the finish line. In a race, runners don't just run in any direction they choose until they get tired or a clock runs out. Instead, there is a clearly marked finish line and designated

Know the goal of your communication!

path between the start and end of the race. Knowing your goal (i.e., finish line) will give you a sense of direction and guide your steps.

To enhance effectiveness, communicators must have a clear goal in mind and develop the content and delivery of their message in a way that best supports reaching their finish line. A runner without a finish line—like a communicator without a goal—is prone to wandering off, going in circles, and venturing into oblivion. At the end, we might say, "Well, I know he was running, but I just don't have any idea where he was going." To avoid someone saying this of you and your communication, always know your goal(s) and then develop and deliver your message accordingly.

NOT ALL GOALS ARE OF EQUAL VALUE

In a given day, your professional interactions may generate any number of communication needs, not all of which will serve your big-picture goals. For instance, on one day you may be working to achieve your bigger communication goals (e.g., increase likability in the office, get support for promotion, or gain sponsorship for new initiative) as well as your smaller, more momentary communication goals (e.g., respond to all those emails or return all those calls). This much is fairly obvious to most. What is often overlooked, however, is that our stated communication goals—big or small—can be easily derailed by "other goals," which may be unspoken and even go unrecognized. Instead, these "other goals" are often revealed by how we treat and react to others. These goals are typically rooted in insecurity or ego needs and are usually easier to spot in others than in ourselves.

There are people who have the need to look competent, so they draft unnecessarily long emails, use big words, and may even take delight in correcting people. Then there are those who have the need to look important, so they needlessly name-drop about others they've been meeting with and look for opportunities to highlight what they've been doing. And, of course, there are people who want to be praised and appreciated for how hard they work, so they find any and all means to appear busy and make references to their impossible workloads and schedules. There are many more examples of these "other goals" and ego needs. But the one thing they have in common is that they notoriously betray our ability to achieve more important goals.

You've likely heard the expression "can't see the forest for the trees." Often, this expression is applied to situations where people have a hard time seeing the big picture because they are too focused on the details of what's right in front of them; they focus on the trees, but don't zoom out to view the whole forest. To be an effective communicator, you must have the presence of mind to recognize your momentary goals and ego needs as well as your big-picture goals (e.g., earn support for a promotion). Take the example of Susanna, a tech lead who was up for promotion to full-time manager, which was her big-picture goal (the forest view). However, Susanna also battled with feeling insecure at work, especially when it came to her technical skills. She feared being compared to her peers and the team that she led, and this insecurity frequently caused her to say and write things that might make her appear more technically advanced than those around her, which was satisfying (albeit, likely ineffectively) her insecurity and momentary needs (the tree view).

We worked on this together for weeks, especially as she was gearing up for a performance evaluation with her manager. We anticipated the questions she might receive and talking points she would need to be in the best position for landing the promotion to manager. In the meeting, when she was asked to describe how a major project was going, the tree perspective was telling her to protect her ego and brag about her technical contribution, but she was prepared and wisely took the forest view and articulated, "The project is going very well for a few reasons. Members of the team are responding well to my leadership style, and we have a good rhythm of work with our partners. The team is very talented, and we are all putting in the time necessary to meet deadlines. I am confident we will get this done ahead of schedule." Where her insecurities and knee-jerk reaction would have led her to focus on her immediate need to be seen as technically superior, quality preparation for the meeting allowed her to keep her focus on her larger goals and better messaging.

And you can do the same. The first step in great preparation is recognizing that you may have momentary goals and ego needs (the tree view), but these may pale in comparison to and can often betray your more important big-picture goals (the forest view).

Let's bring some of this together. Most people agree that effective communication requires proper preparation. I'm adding that preparing well requires that you know and never betray your big-picture goals (the forest perspective) for the sake of getting immediate wins (the tree perspective), some of which are rooted in things like ego and insecurity. In the case of Susanna trying to defend her technical acumen during meetings, she was potentially threatening her bigger goal of becoming a manager. Once she got that sorted out, she was able to demonstrate her leadership potential and managed to earn the promotion she so badly wanted!

Savvy communicators recognize that any given communication is either helping or hindering their ability to achieve larger goals. They get serious about defining their most important goals and then maximize meetings, emails, presentations, and even difficult conversations accordingly. The next critical point on our star is audience, which we explore in Chapter 8.

ESSENTIAL TAKEAWAYS

- Within the first sentence or two of an email or conversation, we want to solve the riddle: "What is the message here, and why does it matter to me?"

- Promise yourself that in every presentation you make and email you send, you are able to finish the sentence, "The purpose of my communication is to_____."

- Communicators must have a clear goal in mind and develop the content and delivery of their message in a way that best supports reaching their finish line.

- Preparation is key to effective communication, and one of the critical parts of being a prepared communicator is to know and never betray your larger professional goals just to gain smaller workplace victories.

CHAPTER 8

Know Your AUDIENCE

Communication Star

Goal

Medium

Audience perception

Messenger

Message

Now that you have defined your communication goal(s), it's time to start focusing on the next point of the star—your audience. The people in your audience are arguably the most important part of your communication equation because they ultimately decide whether you will achieve your goal. Thus, knowledge about your audience and their likely perception of you and your message should be a primary focus as you develop and deliver your communication.

Many individuals fail to realize this, get lazy, or mistakenly presume they are being audience-centered when in actuality they are not.

If you need to know whether your kid is sick, you don't check your own temperature; you check theirs. Similarly, when drafting a letter or preparing for an important meeting or conversation, you don't ask yourself if the message makes sense to you. Instead, you must figure out if the message will make sense to readers or listeners. You put yourself in their shoes. You "check their temperature," and if you don't know the person or people well, you take what you know about them and imagine what the "thermostat in the room" would be, given the message.

Savvy communicators understand that knowing their audience is critical to accomplishing their goal. I once learned this the hard way. An international bank invited me to deliver a four-hour workshop to some of their high-potential managers. Interestingly, the month prior I had given a similar type of talk to a similar type of crowd—*or so I thought*. And because of this poor assumption, I showed up confident that my material from the month prior would work great just the way it was and that I would not need to change much of my message content from one talk to the other. Within 30 minutes, I realized I was completely mistaken when an audience member threw up his hand and said, "The stuff you are sharing is all really good to know, but how does it help me in my actual job? What kind of communication skills can you share with me for what I do?"

He made a bold move, and I am so grateful he did! His question saved the day, and gave me the opportunity to course-correct the workshop in real time, salvage the talk, and win over the crowd. But I nearly lost my audience completely, and it would have been entirely my fault. I was mistakenly giving a great talk to the wrong audience. This situation is a reminder that we must always keep a laser-beam focus on our actual audience. But to do that, you must make time to get out of your own head and see the world through their eyes.

YOUR AUDIENCE DETERMINES YOUR SUCCESS—NOT YOU

Communicators have goals—things they want or need. Ironically, achieving *your* goals as a communicator requires thinking less about yourself and more about your audience. After all, it's your audience that determines your success. So, to develop and deliver effective messages, *spend more time asking what messages your audience needs to receive* and less time focused on what message you want to send.

No matter the industry or role you are in, once people get the sense that you understand them and where they are coming from, odds are they will be warmer to you and your messages. Marcus Cicero (106–43 BC), the famously outspoken Roman politician, is credited with saying, "If you wish to persuade me, you must think my thoughts,

What message does your audience need to receive?

feel my feelings, and speak my words." Even if you aren't selling something and you are merely conveying information, at some level you must persuade your audience of one or a thousand that the information you are sharing is important enough to know, remember, or do something about. You are already persuaded by the content, which is likely why you are sharing it. So, the point is to persuade someone else, and to do that won't require thinking like you; it will require thinking like the audience.

For example, I was recently working with McKenna, a senior product manager from a leading social media company. She was preparing to roll out a technical onboarding roadmap to all impacted teams. She is an incredibly talented individual, but the first draft she brought to me was miserable. I asked about her process for writing it. She thought about it for a moment and responded, "I typed out what we are doing, so they'd know." Her response is typical, and maybe you have also said something similar. Especially when keeping a busy schedule, it's easy to forget to tailor your message for your audience and treat your communications like just another task on the to-do list: pick up laundry; drop off lunch; send companywide announcement.

Next time you have a message to send or an announcement to make, really pause and consider the receiver(s). You probably already know what you want or need from them. But beyond that, consider that you must think like them. Flip your starting line from: "What do I want/need to say?" to "What do they need to hear?" To do this, you will need to have a clear grasp of what they already know, think, and feel about the topic. From there, you will need to get a strong sense of what they do think (or will think) of what you are sharing. If you are seeking alignment and support, is there an obvious incentive for them to align with and support you? You should also evaluate the nature of your relationship—are there any complicated reporting lines or power dynamics involved? What will they think about your method of communicating—will they wish you had chosen a meeting to process and discuss, or will they appreciate that you saved time with an email?

In the case of McKenna who was rolling out the onboarding roadmap, we worked together on a rewrite. I started by having her work with some basic prompts that I encourage you to try:

- What: *The most important thing my audience must know is this . . .*

- So What: *This information is important to my audience because . . .*

- Now What: *This is what my audience can expect for what should/will happen next . . .*

Working through prompts like these will help you get started. In many cases, drafting content that is audience-centered can start and end with those prompts, but in other instances, you may require some additional probing. You may need to go a little deeper and understand where your message fits within your audience's lives. Are they new hires? Disgruntled? Supporters of your cause? Antagonistic toward your team? What is the socio-emotional temperature in the organization? Do these people love the company and its current direction? Are they facing outside pressures or crises? Is this audience hostile to you and your thoughts? Or are they generally warm to you and what you will say?

WHEN YOUR AUDIENCE IS NOT WARM TO YOU OR YOUR IDEAS

For any number of reasons, you may have to prepare a message for an audience that is not warm toward you or your ideas. As you learn more about your audience, you will need to reexamine and potentially redefine your goal. If you initially were planning a proposal for budget money and learn that your vice president has put a clamp on the budget indefinitely, you would be wise to revisit your goal and potentially modify your message accordingly.

I am reminded of a speech by the late Senator Ted Kennedy on "Faith, Truth and Tolerance in America," which he delivered to Liberty Baptist College (now Liberty University).[1] Kennedy, a figurehead of American liberalism, stood before an audience of proud conservatives. The speech is particularly memorable for how Kennedy used humility, honesty, and disarming humor to connect with his audience on what could have been a divisive topic; how he established commonality; and how he effectively accomplished his goal as a communicator. He did not maintain his typical goal of gaining voters for his next presidential run, nor did he go to his normal talking points. Instead, his full awareness of his audience enabled him to develop and deliver a message that accomplished reasonable goals for the occasion.

Few of us give large podium presentations, but even in everyday workplace interaction, we would be wise to learn from his example. Kennedy took the time to put himself in the shoes of the audience—to understand their thoughts and feelings before assuming to impose his own on them. Empathizing with your audience is a requirement for effective communication, especially when your goal is to persuade someone who has opposing views or is on the fence about your topic.

HOW TO HANDLE AUDIENCE CURVEBALLS

Given that your audience is composed of people, and knowing that people are complicated, there is good reason to prepare yourself to be surprised by (and hopefully mitigate) things that may go as you didn't plan. For starters, avoid unnecessary risks with email. Be mindful that when you send a message to one person, your audience could actually be anyone. Email is discoverable and easily shared without consent. Your playful tone with one colleague may not read the same when forwarded to the entire department.

Similar risks occur when on a phone or a virtual call. Just because you don't receive a request to record doesn't mean your audio or video is not being recorded by a nearby device. Likewise, you don't really know who else may be in the room with the other person. I'll never forget being in a conference room when a colleague answered his phone on speaker, saying "What's up?" The immediate reply heard around the room was, "Get this: they are finally going to fire Alicia!" I didn't work there, so it didn't really faze me too much, but guess who was in the room and seemed pretty fazed—Alicia! After having been victim to and witnessed instances of a phone call having more listeners than were presumed, I have a hard rule of always telling the person on the other line if any ears are within earshot (e.g., "Hey Ray, I've got you here on speakerphone with Darlene and Zazil"). I encourage you to practice similar courtesy, but never assume that the same is being done for you.

Additionally, your audience may change on you in a moment, and this may require that you be nimble and pivot. I am sure you have wondered a time or two, *Why are they in this meeting?* In some instances, it may be wise to stay the course. In other cases, you need to figure out real fast how this change in audience impacts your goals (will you need to refine them?) and messaging.

For example, Liberty is a client of mine who does food and beverage product marketing. She was preparing for a standing meeting with her director, which is when they regularly run through progress and updates, but this time she was going to confide to him that there was turmoil on the team and ask for his support managing the situation. She dreaded having to share this but wanted to get ahead of the issue and have his support, rather than have anything escalate further or deadlines missed.

They were 10 minutes into the meeting, and she was just about to share her concerns with him, when unexpectedly her team barged in to get some quick feedback about a nonurgent decision. Liberty and her director proceeded to give her team some direction, but Liberty decided to capitalize on the barging in. Following the discussion around the nonurgent decision, Liberty said, "While we are all here with our director, I wanted to give a quick shout-out to the team . . . " and then proceeded to acknowledge some recent achievements. She followed by adding a small word of challenge, outlining the obstacles ahead and acknowledging ways the team was going to have to grow together in order to really build upon past success. She rightfully impressed herself in that moment.

The next day her director called her and complimented her on how well she was managing the team and pledged his support however she needed as they moved forward, especially given the bumps they were managing on the team. What I love about how Liberty managed the situation is that she didn't let her change of audience derail her ability to achieve her goal. In fact, she even managed to get more out of the moment, not less. If Liberty had stuck to her script that was geared specifically for her boss (e.g., "Well, since you all are in here, I guess it's good you hear this too . . .") the meeting could have resulted in a major blowup, which could have been damaging for both her and her team. Instead, she had the presence of mind to let her circumstances shape and mold her message, achieving her goal and more.

We may not always be so lucky, but no matter the situation we must always be willing to pivot and adapt when presented with a change in audience or situation. Other times, we must read the situation and redefine our goals and what success will mean. A while back I was invited to do a content-heavy keynote for a midsized tech firm. It was their annual company retreat held at a fancy resort. I had never worked with them before, but from all the instructions I was given and thorough planning on their part, I arrived with an expectation that this would be a very formal event.

However, when I arrived, I soon realized this was not going to be the case. My point of contact greeted me and was moving a bit sluggishly. Her boss, the president of the company, arrived to meet me as well and appeared to be soothing a sunburn. More people showed up with breakfast and mimosas in hand. Lots of board shorts and ball caps. One guy asked if anyone had Advil.

They clearly didn't want a content-heavy keynote. They wanted some fun and a farewell song. So I threw out my prepared presentation and played the court jester for 90 minutes. Everyone had a blast, including me.

The reason everything worked out OK is twofold. First, before a big meeting or presentation, read the room not your notes. Remember, these people decide whether you reach your goal. Second, remain nimble and allow your goal to change as needed.

Taking an audience-centered approach reminds us that one of our greatest communication muscles to cultivate is listening. Savvy communicators look and listen for cues from the person or people they are interacting with. They pay attention to nuance and listen for unspoken messages during meetings. They remain present and in the moment to ensure they don't just hear words but truly understand what is happening around them.

There are many reasons people fail to grow their listening muscles. For one, it's easy to shortchange active listening by daydreaming and multitasking. Likewise, in a world desperately trying to convince us that we are each the center of the universe, to listen is to acknowledge that we are not.

LISTENING IS CORE TO COMMUNICATING EFFECTIVELY

I run nearly every day yet seldom do core exercises. But every active runner knows that strengthening your core is critical to improving as a runner. In a communication paradigm, I liken active listening to core exercises. Most people talk every day yet struggle with active listening. But, just as one's core is critical to running, strengthening your active listening skills is critical to communicating effectively. With some intentionality, we can all grow active listening muscles.

Listening is the *active process* of *making meaning* out of another person's spoken message.[2] I intentionally emphasize listening as an *active process* because it doesn't happen automatically. Listening is a choice and can be a hard one to make in our world of limitless distraction. I also emphasize listening is a process of *making meaning* because when we realize the reason we listen at all is to understand, we can see our conversations in a completely different light.

Imagine sitting in a team meeting and your coworker, Jack, volunteers to take the lead on yet another project. Because you've known him for three years, you recognize that he's volunteering because his goal is to stack his résumé for the promotion that he wants to earn later this quarter. But another colleague who isn't as close to Jack hears this and makes a note to encourage him to not take on this additional work after the meeting because it could result in burnout. Yet another colleague was replying to his inbox during the discussion, so he heard

Strengthening your active listening skills
is critical to communicating effectively

only bits and pieces of the interaction. Everyone in the meeting physically heard what transpired, but their listening was impacted by their personal situations.

One person was not actively listening, as he was too distracted by his own inbox. One was actively listening and managed to make sense of the message, albeit different from Jack's intent because he lacked the necessary context. And you were actively listening and established shared meaning with Jack because you had the necessary context. That being said, shared meaning does not necessarily mean both people agree about what should happen. For instance, you might also think Jack could burn out if he takes on this new project, but you understand he did it because he is striving for the promotion.

We have several barriers to effective listening, including:

- *Noise* from your own devices or the nearby table is being so loud that it literally distracts you from catching critical messages in the meeting you are attending.

- *Information overload* from a prior meeting or competing thoughts in your head prevent you from being fully present.

- *Pseudo-listening* and *glazing over* occur when a speaker's message is unclear or does not captivate your attention and you proceed to daydream.

- *Closed-mindedness* and *rebuttal tendency* are when you refuse to listen or do so only to *interrupt* and argue, which prevents you from actively listening for understanding and establishing connectedness with the speaker.

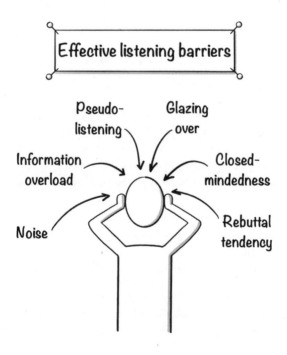

Effective listening barriers

Pseudo-listening

Glazing over

Information overload

Closed-mindedness

Noise

Rebuttal tendency

Whatever the barrier is that's stopping you from active and effective listening, it's important to identify and strive to eliminate whatever is hindering you from being a better listener. An active listener is one who remains sincerely engaged with others. Active listeners mentally recognize, sort, re-sort, and rephrase key information. Given that a person can usually hear and listen to messages faster than a speaker can say them, the temptation for most listeners is to multitask, when instead, they should focus on interpreting all that is (and is not) being communicated.

As a simple suggestion, when deemed appropriate, keep a pen and pad nearby during meetings. This is helpful for multiple reasons. When competing thoughts flood your head, especially something you are afraid you will forget, just jot it down real quick and actively reorient your attention to the meeting you are in. Likewise, if the person speaking is failing to capture your attention, yet you know it is important to stay focused on the speaker and the message, jot down key phrases and see if you can reconstruct the outline of the message on paper. This will force you to focus critically on the message, even when difficult to do so. There are two reasons I suggest using a pen and pad rather than a device. First, the device is likely to tempt you further away from the present moment and draw your attention to competing applications. Second, whereas others are likely to assume you are actively listening when taking handwritten notes, people are more likely to assume you are distracted if you are glancing at a device.

USE THE HURIER MODEL

One way to become a better listener is to implement the HURIER model—Hear, Understand, Remember, Interpret, Evaluate, and

Respond. This is a proven method used to help individuals actively listen.[3] Let's break down each step:

1. **Hear:** The first step toward listening better is ensuring you can actually *hear* others well, by limiting noise and distraction. You can also set yourself up for success by being intentional when picking times and places to meet with others. For instance, a critical conversation with your manager that requires people hear one another well and remain focused may best be saved for a quiet office, rather than at a popular restaurant during lunch hour.

2. **Understand:** To *understand* the speaker is to (un)consciously process and understand the words being spoken. Language barriers, cultural norms, and technical jargon can often cause uncertainty or misunderstanding. If you don't understand or feel uncertain about what a speaker is saying, it's far better to check for understanding than make a costly or preventable error. Although people sometimes feel intimidated or embarrassed when needing to check for comprehension, restating to ensure complete understanding and asking questions to clarify intentions are two important steps that are worth taking. Another step to try is to offer a meeting recap or send a follow-up note to ensure mutual understanding (e.g., "From what I heard, I understand *x*. Given this, we are planning to do *x*. Are we aligned on that?").

3. **Remember:** *Remembering* may either be done through mindfulness in the moment or literally taking notes on what is said, in order that the message can be recalled and

acted upon. Many people grow up trying various mnemonic devices (e.g., the treble staff in music "EGBDF" is often remembered using the phrase "Every Good Boy Does Fine") or other tricks for remembering study material. Additionally, you can try a trick that many public figures learn early in their careers: when first meeting someone, casually incorporate his or her name into the first few moments of the interaction to increase the odds you will remember the name throughout the conversation and beyond.

4. **Interpret:** *Interpreting* is when we make sense of the verbal, nonverbal, and contextual aspects of the message. Sometimes messages are not straightforward, such as when people use sarcasm. To effectively interpret messages, we must listen for and observe all the data points available to us. With just a subtle eye roll, eyebrow flash, or smirk, the phrase "I had a great time" may be interpreted a number of ways. When a message has been misinterpreted, it is often the job of the message sender to clarify the proper interpretation (e.g., "Actually, I am being serious" or "I was just kidding"). If it is an important topic and the person speaking is not communicating clearly or being forthright and you need to get an accurate interpretation, it may be wise to casually seek out additional input from alternative sources.

5. **Evaluate:** *Evaluating* is where we assign value to the message, determining things like how important or applicable we believe the message to be. In order to evaluate messages wisely, it is important to distinguish between emotional appeals and logical arguments, as well as recognizing the

influence of personal bias. Another helpful tip is to try differentiating the ideas presented from the person speaking. You can do this by asking yourself if (or how) your evaluation of this information would change if it were presented by someone else.

6. **Respond:** *Responding* is giving feedback verbally or nonverbally. You can respond to others any number of ways by a head nod, tears, laughter, verbal utterance (e.g., hmm, ahhh, "OK," "I see"), paraphrasing the message, asking follow-up questions, or giving advice. You may even choose to stonewall, which is to respond with silence. Importantly, there is not a right response for all situations. Instead, the right response will be one that suits your goal, audience, and situation best.

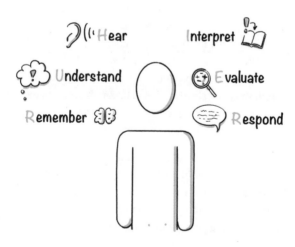

To begin improving your listening, I recommend jotting down the HURIER model and remembering it next time you enter a meeting so you can be mindful of doing each step. Listening is a critical workplace skill, and practicing the right techniques is the best bet for improving.

Listening well can strengthen our relationships at work and beyond. Listening is not only an important skill designed to respect and dignify those around us. It's also a smart strategy for those who wish to learn and leverage the best of others' ideas and for those wise enough to preserve their political and social capital on the ideas they actually need to speak to. I'd rather be the guy about whom people say, "When he speaks, I listen," than the guy about whom they say, "He's always got something to say."

When we don't listen well, our communication and relationships suffer. Listening intently to others, even when you don't agree with what is being said, sends a positive and confirming message.

Finally, remember that active listening does not equal endorsing a message. You can disagree with a colleague's recommendation, yet in the spirit of being a good colleague, you can demonstrate through active listening that you recognize and acknowledge the person as well as his or her point of view. Attentive eyes, a warm smile, and a head nod doesn't necessarily mean you agree, it can just mean you care enough to listen. This is an important way to show others we value them and desire to work together well, even when we hold differing viewpoints.

ESSENTIAL TAKEAWAYS

- Knowledge about your audience and likely perception of you and your message should be your primary focus as you develop and deliver your communication.

- Listening is the *active process* of *making meaning* out of another person's spoken message.

- Barriers to effective listening include noise, information overload, pseudo-listening, glazing over, closed-mindedness, rebuttal tendency, and interruptions.

- One way to become a better listener is to implement the HURIER model—Hear, Understand, Remember, Interpret, Evaluate, and Respond.

- Listening well can strengthen our relationships at work and beyond.

CHAPTER

9

Own Your MESSAGE

Communication Star

Goal

Audience
perception

Medium

Messenger   **Message**

After you've defined and refined your communication goals (as discussed in Chapter 7), conducted due diligence on your audience, and begun to focus on active listening (both discussed in Chapter 8), it is time to begin thinking about how to develop and deliver a winning message. We're now ready to wonder: *What should I say?*

The messages you send are either working for you or against you. This can be true for any number of communication events—presentations, high-stake meetings, interviews, difficult conversations, and the list goes on! This chapter focuses on mastering the essentials for developing clear, concise, and compelling messages that are structured to have maximum impact.

THE CHALLENGE WITH OWNING YOUR MESSAGE

Most of us want to be effective communicators. We want our messages to be influential and have impact. Doing so requires effort—not only sometimes, but all the time, because every day we are faced with new opportunities to either own our messages or just manage them. No matter how familiar your workday seems, going into autopilot with your communication is a bad idea. Today is an opportunity for you to achieve your personal and professional goals by elevating your communications.

There are a few things that may stand in your way of being able to communicate most effectively. Some people may lack the know-how for delivering impactful messages. Others may have the know-how but lack the conviction to put forth the effort. For those of you who lack the conviction or believe you don't have time to craft better content or prepare for meetings, I encourage you to think about the opportunities you may be missing, both in the moment and in the future. Not prioritizing how you manage your everyday communications can be costly. You can be doing all the right things at work and even be producing the best ideas, but you may still fail to earn your next promotion or be given the next great opportunity if you aren't communicating your ideas or the impact of your work effectively.

Developing clear, concise, and compelling messages is important not only when preparing for the next podium presentation. You should be striving for clear, concise, and compelling messages when meeting with your manager, when sending a memo to your team, when preparing for your next client call, and in many other business communication situations.

One reason why writing a clear, concise, and compelling message may be challenging for you in the workplace is because you know *too* much about the topic at hand! People don't ask for your point of view on things you know little about; instead, they expect you to speak up on those things you think about and deal with every day. For example, if someone asked me to do a presentation on the basics of baseball—a sport I know very little about—it would almost be a fun challenge. Starting from zero, I'd call some people, learn a few things, and then start developing my message. It wouldn't be very impressive, but I certainly wouldn't feel overwhelmed by the task or spin in circles with what to say.

Conversely, if someone asked me to talk about running—something I do nearly every day—it would be more challenging. I'd be working with a web of information and memories and trying to sort them into clear and concise thoughts. I might even second-guess myself about whether I was sharing the most important information or wonder if my message lived up to expectations, given I should know something about this topic. I describe this challenge as knowing how to find just the right cup of water from an ocean of information, because you aren't short of content to pull from, but it can also get overwhelming when you have too much information to swim through.

Chances are, unless you are new to your role, you experience this challenge also. When you are asked to give an update, send a memo, make a pitch, and so on, the responsibility to bear the message did not fall on you because you know little about the subject (e.g., like me with baseball), but instead it's your message to craft and share because you know and/or care so much (e.g., like me with running). In the case of crafting a memo or leading a discussion on a big topic, the solution is to *focus on your audience* rather than the sea of information you are swimming in. When you start with your audience and think through what they must know, you can then quickly sort through your knowledge bank to find the precise content to share. Not doing so just leads to the proverbial data dump.

To illustrate the point, I'd like to have you over to my house. Imagine a Sunday afternoon. Our family has just returned from brunch, and I walk back to my daughters' room. All over the floor, huge piles of clothes are tossed about and left out. It's a huge mess. Only a skilled gymnast could enter this room without landing on heaps of clothing. I encourage my daughters to clean up their room and put all their clothes away. A few minutes later, I return to their room and, to my pleasant surprise, discover that there are no clothes on the floor! But as I open their drawers, they're all crammed full of unfolded clothes, making it impossible to distinguish one item from another.

Many times, when I read an email or sit through a business presentation, I wonder if the author or speaker is doing to his or her message what my daughters do with their clothes: take whatever they've got and cram it in somewhere else.

When you receive emails or memos like this, it can feel like the person writing them thought, *You want me to send out an update on the status of the project? Sure, let me just type everything that comes to my mind in one long stream-of-conscious and then click send.*

Almost anyone can take piles of information and move them from one spot to another. I bet without thinking too hard about it, you can recall a recent memo you've received or a meeting you've sat through that left you thinking, *OK, to make any sense of this, I need a cup of coffee and an hour to organize this information.* Just like the clothes in the drawer, you'll need to go back to sort through it all to make any sense of what's what.

When this happens, the messenger has done you no favors—merely checking the box and delivering you a big messy pile of information. My hope is that you never commit such a crime.

No matter how vast your ocean of information or how messy your pile of clothes, with the right tools you can develop a winning message. The remainder of this chapter shows you how to do exactly that: to develop an audience-centered message that is always three things: *clear*, *concise*, and *compelling*.

Don't cram your messages with big, messy piles of information

BE CLEAR

Clarity matters. And it doesn't only matter if the message is clear or makes sense to you. With clear communication as one of your critical objectives, the hope is that those who receive your message would think to themselves, *Wow, I totally get it. Thanks for helping me make sense of this.*

To achieve this, you must thoughtfully package ideas and information and deliver them in a way that helps your audience easily understand what is being conveyed. A.G. Lafley, former CEO of Procter and Gamble, is known for insisting that messages be "*Sesame Street* Simple."[1] He wisely understood that people don't want to work hard to understand you. It's your job to do the hard work of making your message easily understandable. Still, I know many people struggle with keeping their message simple and delivering it in the "Sesame Street" version. For some, the simple truth is that they don't actually understand the material. So how could they possibly break it down simply for others? Another common struggle is about ego and the fear of sounding so simple that others would think *you* are simple or lack intelligence because you don't use big words. In this case, I highly urge you to rethink your strategy.

In all the cases I can think of, speaking simply and with clarity proves quite the opposite. You'd much rather be a communicator who simplifies the complex rather than being the one who complicates what should have been simple.

Your message matters, but only to the extent that your audience can understand it. To increase understanding of your message, make sure you are using language that is concrete (not vague or abstract), active (rather than passive), grammatically correct, and easy to follow. Even still, there are times when knowledge gaps or differing opinions may cause others to not clearly receive your message. Here is when you should consider employing analogous language such as metaphors, similes, and parables.

For example, imagine having to explain LinkedIn to people who have never seen or used it. You could describe each and every feature, hoping they would somehow catch on to what you are saying. Or, if knowing they have Facebook accounts, you could simply say, "Well, it's like the Facebook for professional networking." With just a few simple words and by tapping into what is known (e.g., Facebook), you can help others imagine something that may be unknown, in this case, LinkedIn. This gives you a starting line to then compare, contrast, and dive deeper into the topic as necessary.

If your job involves communicating with individuals who may not have your technical expertise or depth of understanding, I strongly advise developing a list of analogous examples that you can employ, depending on with whom you are interacting, to help you establish a shared base line of information to work from.

There are other times when people understand the logic clearly, but need gripping analogous language to help them experience the *why* more clearly. For example, I recently worked with a client who was trying to get buy-in to invest in a corporate social responsibility plan for a video-streaming platform. She was proposing her company invest resources to make the platform accessible to vision-impaired individuals and provide additional security so that young viewers would not be at risk of being exposed to adult content. She knew there would be resistance to her ideas, but leaning into some language from her company's mission statement, we developed a message that went something like this:

> Our platform is rays of sunshine for people everywhere. Our opportunity is to ensure that vision-impaired people have access to those rays and that young viewers are protected from rays that could harm them.

Mastering the metaphor saves time, helps you own the message, and layers your message with additional clarity, which brings us back to the main point: being speaker-centered means telling people your big idea clearly and quickly; never making your audience work hard to understand you.

BE CONCISE

If being clear means ensuring that what you're talking about is simplified and understandable, then being concise means ensuring you talk about the right things—and nothing else. When you are knowledgeable and care a great deal about your subject, it can be especially difficult to focus your content on only the most important information. All those nifty tidbits of information that fascinate you can cause your colleagues and clients to tune you out.

I observed this on a recent trip with my mom to the car dealership. As we approached the car she liked, an associate rushed over to us. We had high hopes that he could help us to quickly determine if this car would be "the one." From my perspective, he had about a minute or less before we were going to decide whether we wanted to keep talking to him.

Now, put yourself in this salesperson's shoes for a moment. Given his audience (a mother and her adult son), the context (it was August in the heat of south Texas), and any other critical factors, what would you have chosen to focus on and point out first when making your sales pitch?

Well, you might be thinking to emphasize the air-conditioning and how the car cools down really fast by saying something like, "Go ahead. Have a seat, and let's get the air-conditioning cranked up." But that's not what happened. Instead, the first features he decided to point out to my mom were the superb sound system and how quickly the seats heat, followed by a long list of vehicle details that would have fascinated my daughter much more than my mother. Needless to say, we got out of there quick and found another dealership with salespeople who knew better than to waste our time.

What can we learn from this story? Audience-centered messages are clear and concise. Audience-centered communicators quickly zero in on what the listener must know.

A mentor of mine used to keep a replica of a dartboard that he would show to his employees. The outer ring read *nice to know*, the middle ring read *should know*, and the innermost ring (i.e., bull's-eye) read *must know*. He often reminded people entering his office for a meeting, "We've only got half an hour, so let's start with the bull's-eye. What must I know?"

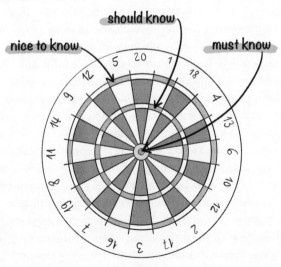

There's no need for you to go out and buy a dartboard, but I'd encourage you to keep that image in mind when thinking of how to target your message and maximize time. *Speaker-centered* communicators communicate from their own perspective and talk about whatever they want. In contrast, an *audience-centered* communicator is laser-beam-focused on crafting messages that are clear and concise for the recipient. A great rule of thumb is: You do not need to tell people everything you know! To be audience-centered means telling people what they must know, not all the neat and nifty things you happen to know.

STRUCTURE SMARTER

A critical step toward making your content clearer and more concise is to structure your content with the audience in mind versus yourself as the messenger. Most of us structure our communications (whether via email, memo, one-on-one conversation, small meeting group, or large on-stage speech) as a *funnel*—with the information presented first and the main point (the big "ta-da" moment) at the end. In doing this, we basically dump information and force the listener/reader to determine what part of our message is meaningful. Your audience shouldn't have to read your thousand-word email or listen to your entire pitch before understanding why anything you're sharing matters.

Instead, you need to flip the funnel and communicate like a pyramid, beginning with the main point and then providing necessary tidbits of information to help your audience process and sort the information you're sharing. Doing this makes your key insights, main points, big takeaways, and solutions take the main stage at the start of your presentation. In turn, this allows others to focus on what is most important as they receive the additional evidence to explain what you

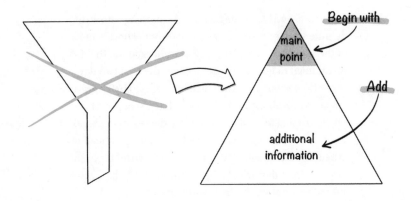

are recommending, why it is the right recommendation, and how it will work.

Smarter structure is something that you can practice in everyday interactions. In fact, practicing smart structure in low-stakes communication is what makes structuring smarter more natural in high-stakes situations.

Don't be that colleague who spends 10 minutes building up a story, explaining unnecessary details of information, all to leave peers hanging until the very end for a big reveal or ending that wasn't all that exciting by the time that colleague got there. And don't be the colleague who drafts incredibly long emails that require people to read the entirety before reaching any call to action until the very end. Imagine you are at the airport and your colleague calls to tell you:

> Luke came by the office . . . turns out he has a dental appointment tomorrow around 11 a.m. that could last the rest of the day. . . . Andy called to let us know that he got

pulled into an SLT meeting tomorrow morning with an indefinite start time, so he is going to be out of pocket most of the morning. . . . Also, Andrew messaged me that he might need to be on site with a client the next two days, something about an audit which he seems to believe you already knew about. . . . And, lastly, Matt just popped by to say he is going to go ahead and work the rest of this week from home. His partner returned from Europe ahead of schedule, and he said that you would understand. . . . So, yeah, quite a day around here. And with all that, what should we do about Ruth's farewell party?

The information here is pretty clear and relatively concise, but the structure is a mess. It runs chronologically and requires the listener to focus too hard on determining what is meaningful and how best to sort the information. It is what happens when we deliver information like a funnel—a flow of events that makes you get all the way to the end before knowing why any of it matters. Imagine the same call went like this: "We may need to rethink the timing of Ruth's farewell party. Luke, Andy, Andrew, and Matt have all confirmed they will miss tomorrow due to varying schedule conflicts. I've got the details on each if you want them."

Many people take a "funnel" approach when it comes to delivering a message—sharing tidbits of information that eventually lead to a main point. This is problematic because it doesn't focus on the *audience* and how they can receive information most effectively. Audience-centered communicators do the opposite. They deliver messages like a pyramid, beginning with the main point and then provide necessary tidbits of information to help their audience process and sort the information in a way that's not just easier to digest, but more effective, too.

To use the pyramid approach, you must first set the stage by quickly reminding the audience why you are there (e.g., on the stage, in the meeting, or in their inbox). Follow this with your big idea, perhaps the solution to the problem. Next, back up the idea by letting them know your recommendation is supported by main points, each of which have data to support your big idea. And at the end, just for good measure, always bookend the content—in other words, the ending ought to reinforce the core message.

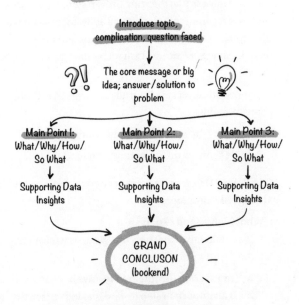

The Pyramid Approach to Structuring Smarter Communications

Here's a detailed example of how I helped Vikas, a DevOps client, address a hotly contested issue at work and present on it using a pyramid structure:

- **Introduction (state the problem):**
  "We've had ongoing conversations about the challenges surrounding our security authorization. Related to this, our audit necessitates we get serious about resolving this issue immediately."

- **Core Message (present your proposed solution):**
  "The good news is that there are proven steps we can take. And those recommended steps will allow for easier engineer onboarding, scaling of our infrastructure, and better security and reliability. Specifically, I am recommending we do the following:

  1. Remove admin access from all engineers in existing environments.

  2. Work with IT to create new authorization groups.

  3. Provide short-term/temporary permissions."

- **Main Point #1: Remove admin access from all engineers in existing environments.**

  - **What (define and explain):**
    "This would mean that only one group is left with admin rights."

  - **Why (motivation/problem to resolve):**
    "This is an important step toward making ourselves compliant and would align us more closely with best practices."

○ **How (necessary steps, what it would take to get it done):**
"This will require auditing engineers with admin rights, communicating with the engineers, and moving those engineers into a newer group.

"In just a moment, I'll give a rundown of what I mean by 'newer groups,' but on this point of removing admin access, I am proposing we follow a strict timeline that will give engineers ample time to adapt to the changes coming."

○ **So what impact (emphasizing the future state):**
"Taking these steps will mean the primary user will be the only user who is able to deploy to the production environment.

"And one point to consider is that the incident response might be more difficult for engineers, as they will need to request temporary elevated permissions for some actions (which we can discuss momentarily).

"The benefits of this change, however, will also mean that we will have a better ability to audit production code changes."

• **Main Point #2 (Repeat process for "Work with IT to create new authorization groups.")**

• **Main Point #3 (Repeat process for "Provide short-term/ temporary permissions.")**

• **Conclusion:**
"Given the current state and challenges we face, this proven and implementable recommendation is our best choice going forward. In addition to mitigating risks and following best practices, taking these necessary steps gets us closer to

our important goal of compliance. I am grateful for your time today, and I welcome any questions you may have."

The good news for Vikas is that he got the green light on his proposed recommendation. In fact, following this meeting, his manager asked him to start giving more updates during senior leadership meetings. So, a word of caution to you: elevating your communication skills usually leads to more communication opportunities!

Chances are that you may not speak the technical language from this example! I don't either. The point of the example isn't that you implement a security authorization. It's that you dissect the structure and style and try it for yourself with your next memo, status update, or recommendation. The pyramid structure forces us to keep our message clear and concise, improving the probability that we will captivate others and inspire them to think, feel, and behave a particular way.

BE COMPELLING

To compel is to evoke interest and persuade. A compelling argument is one that cannot be easily refuted. Think of a courtroom, where a witness provides compelling testimony that persuades jurors toward a particular verdict. However, what compels you may not compel your colleague. So, when considering how to compel others, I encourage people to consider the primary persuasive appeals. There are logical appeals, emotional appeals, and then appeals to things like character and credibility

If you learn that your manager is compelled by logic and numbers, then you would want to always include data when presenting your ideas to your boss:

We've got to do something about this. Look at the number of young people affected by this. The numbers don't lie. It's time we make a change.

Then there are others who are less persuaded by sheer numbers, but they are persuaded by someone who seems credible or trustworthy. For them, you might say something like:

I spoke with our head of finance about projected revenues. She is persuaded that our customer-retention program will not eat into margins and that it even shows promise for improving long-term shareholder value creation. Given that we have a green light from her, I recommend we move forward.

Even still, some are less persuaded by spreadsheets or white coats and are persuaded more by emotional appeals. Most marketing techniques incorporate some form of emotional appeal to everyday consumers, but appealing to emotion is also important within the workplace. You may choose to appeal to your organization's mission and principles by saying something like:

The decision to double our efforts in order to meet this customer deadline isn't only about getting paid; it's about honoring the very principles that this company was founded on. If we are truly customer-obsessed, we don't pick and choose when to serve the customer. If we are truly customer-obsessed, then what are we complaining about? This is more than just doing a job. This is about fulfilling a mission.

An important thing to note here is that your writing and speaking should not utilize one appeal (e.g., logic, credibility, or emotion) exclusively. In fact, you are better off combining all three as often as you can. This is especially true when you are less familiar with your audience, as you have yet to learn the appeals that tend to compel them.

Remember: just because a message or idea compels you does not mean that it compels your audience. So in picking your appeals, stay laser-focused on your intended audience. A couple of summers ago, while I was doing some Saturday morning chores with the family, there was a loud and unexpected knock at the front door. I opened the door to a young man I didn't know, so I asked, "Hi, how can I help you?"

He said, "Ya, you want to buy some magazines?"

I answered honestly: "Um, no. Not really."

That led him to his "sales pitch": "I need to sell these magazines. It'll help me reach my numbers. If I reach my numbers, I'm going to get a bonus check."

I felt sorry for him . . . but I had no desire to buy any magazines, so I gave him $5 to get lunch.

Because my field is communication, though, I couldn't help reflecting on how ineffective his sales pitch was: Did he appeal to *me* in any way? No. I suppose he provided logic about something that appealed to him: if *he* reached his sales goal, *he* would get a bonus check. That's a lousy speaker-centered pitch. Yet it's a mistake any of us are capable of making.

A better approach would have been for him (and any salesperson) to survey everything he possibly could while approaching my home, quickly size up the residents, and say:

> Hello sir. Sorry to bother you on the weekend, but I am
> in your neighborhood offering you and your neighbors

incredible pricing on some of the world's most popular magazines. Your neighbor just ordered a year of this *Golf Digest* right here. I saw the running shoes on your steps and am guessing you might want to hear about deals on this *Running Digest*. The baby swing out front tells me you might also be interested in this *Parenting Journal*. Again, I don't mean to take too much time, but would you give me just one minute so I can tell you about our best-in-class reputation and unbeatable pricing?

I can't promise that this revised approach would have worked, but the audience-centered style would have been far more impressive and would have caused more people—including me!—to hear him out. Remember, *you* don't decide if you reach your goal, your audience does. Just because an idea compels *you* does not mean it compels *your audience*. The odds of compelling the listener are in your favor when you keep your focus on your audience.

Your ideas won't appeal to everyone. In fact, many people are bombarded with ideas, and so they are at once turned off at the thought of another one. For this reason, I urge you to not begin an email, phone call, or presentation by saying, "I have an idea that I want to share." The magazine salesperson had an idea: "If you buy some magazines, it will help me reach my numbers." But his idea didn't appeal to me at all.

Here's another example of how important it is to communicate in a more compelling way. One of my clients recently received a really poor performance evaluation, and my gut tells me it wasn't necessarily his fault. His company uses a standard rubric to grade its territories. If you are below the average, then your evaluation will reflect it. All year long he was above average, and then the last few months, his territory tanked. So many external factors could explain why, but his manager didn't see it that way. And unfortunately, my client didn't respond in a clear, concise, or compelling way. His ego got the best of him, he got defensive, and his messaging to his manager during their meeting could have nearly gotten him fired.

We had a long talk about how to salvage things. He, of course, was focused on salvaging his lost bonus. I was more concerned with him keeping his job! (Still feeling a bit emotional, I don't think he fully grasped that he had been put on a serious performance improvement plan.) We determined that he needed to request a follow-up meeting where he could try to salvage his relationship with his manager in addition to his career. We talked extensively about how he could build a message using a pyramid structure that included more than one appeal. Knowing that he lost his bonus due to numbers and logic, we needed to use numbers and logic to make a case for his potential. Also, since he demonstrated negative emotion during his evaluation meeting, we built in positive emotion that hinted at institutional principles. In the end, he got his evaluation score up a whole point (from a two to a three out of five), which meant a teeny-tiny bonus—and he was taken off his performance improvement plan two months later.

Let's tie some of this together. You want strong content with strong structure to support it, and you must be laser-focused on your audience and how they will receive you and your message. You'd never write a love letter "to whom it may concern." Likewise, your professional messages are to real humans who are asking themselves, *What's in this for me?* If you're developing content and structure with the audience in mind, you're well on your way to successful communication.

I've been told by many senior leaders that they have little time for listening to new ideas. They've got ideas piled up high all over their desks. But you know what they need? They need people who can spot and solve preexisting problems. So I dare you to take your next nifty idea and repackage it as a solution to a preexisting problem. If you don't remind people of the problem being solved and the pain being alleviated by your solution, your grand thought or big idea is all too easy to ignore, delete, or just leave on the dusty bookshelf of forgotten ideas.

Imagine the person you're communicating with has a big headache. To walk in declaring your lofty ideas, unaware of the person's pain, is potentially adding to the inflammation. Conversely, to be audience-centered means discovering how your idea can be the ibuprofen to the headache.

ANTICIPATE AND REFUTE THE REBUTTAL

One way to prevent a headache is by anticipating any natural rebuttal to your idea or suggestion and facing it head on. Ask yourself, *What will be the rebuttal to what I am sharing?* Where some communicators try to run from the resistance and play ignorant to the probable obstacles they will face from others, I highly advise that you instead run *through* the resistance with well-timed refutation strategies. It serves you better to refute rebuttals than to be forced to address them awkwardly during a question-and-answer period or future meeting.

For example, one of my clients is a director of engineering for a cloud-based software company. He was determined to get buy-in from senior leaders for a multimillion-dollar overhaul of computer equipment that would benefit every engineer in the organization. His timing was awful. It was the height of a pandemic and company stock was down. He hadn't done a great job preselling the idea, and his company's expectation for a proposal of this size was that it needed to be drafted and distributed as a well-formulated proposal, followed with a formal presentation and discussion of the proposal.

During our work developing and rehearsing his message, I was really struggling with how to help him increase the odds of winning favor from decision makers. Then he shared with me that it was funny for him to be making this pitch given that he had been completely opposed to the idea just a few months earlier. I asked him to explain, and he told me all the reasons he was against this idea and how his own view had changed after scouring the data and interviewing engineers. I said, "That's it! That's your presentation." We ended up developing a 15-minute presentation entirely around refuting the most obvious rebuttals to his proposal, and we jokingly titled it "Why I Changed My Mind and Why You Should, Too."

His previous version was very stuffy and felt like watching someone push a rock uphill. When he acknowledged the most obvious rebuttals and used his most compelling points as refutation, it allowed him to present an authentic message with ease. In the end, he got the money and was promoted six months later. The engineers still sing his praises!

The critical takeaway is that by developing messages that are clear, concise, and compelling, and account for the resistance and rebuttals of your audience, you will be more likely to achieve your communication goals in the workplace and beyond.

While this chapter focused heavily on crafting winning content, the next chapter takes a closer look at how communication essentials enable us to deliver with confidence.

ESSENTIAL TAKEAWAYS

- When you focus on your audience and think through what *they* must know, you can quickly sort through what *you* know to find the precise content to share.

- Think of a pyramid rather than a funnel when organizing your ideas. Start with your main point and then add necessary information to help your audience process and sort the information you're sharing.

- You can compel your audience to act in three ways: by using logic (and data that supports your ideas), by proving credibility and trustworthiness, and by appealing to their emotions. Try to use all three.

- Keep in mind those you are communicating with when you craft your message. Ask yourself, *What's in this for them?*

- Anticipate how your audience might respond to and refute your ideas. If you're prepared for their arguments, you can more easily refute them and win over your audience to your ideas.

CHAPTER
10

Anticipate How Your Audience Will Perceive You, the MESSENGER

Communication Star

Goal

Audience perception

Medium

Message

Messenger

Previous chapters have emphasized the importance of knowing your goal, being audience-centered, and managing the message. This chapter focuses on you and your ability to deliver messages with impact. Truthfully, I get a little alarmed when someone wants my help preparing a slide deck and talk track but insists that there is no time to rehearse the delivery. You absolutely must invest time in mastering your content, but not at the peril of delivering it well. This is because people don't merely buy things and ideas; they buy the messenger of those things and ideas. This is true of social media influencers, brand ambassadors, and presidential candidates, and it is true of you.

Whether you are preparing to speak in an upcoming meeting, make a client call, or deliver a lengthy presentation, you are the voice and face of that message. Your idea won't sell itself. You must manage both your content and delivery. This chapter focuses on communication essentials to help you establish credibility and convey confidence through your vocal and visual delivery.

BOTH CONTENT AND DELIVERY ARE CRITICAL

Have you ever thought or said something like, "There isn't time to rehearse the content. I already know this material. I just need to get the deck put together and make sure the information looks right." If so, think again. It's not an either/or. Effective communicators don't decide between content or delivery, they master both.

We can learn from my client who founded two San Francisco startups that failed and now focuses his efforts on investing in fintech and advising entrepreneurs. He helps new founders learn from his mistakes—one of the most important being that he never wanted to rehearse his communication. His thinking was that it was more important to be his authentic, in-the-moment self. This may have worked well with some of his core team, but it didn't work with potential investors. When asked by investors why he was the right person to lead the company, he would sheepishly share that he wasn't sure he was the right person, but that he would do his very best and always be honest. His authenticity was admirable, but he failed to instill the confidence necessary to propel his companies forward because he didn't rehearse and polish his communication delivery. It's admirable to present authentically, but not at the expense of instilling confidence in those around you.

If you really want to engender followership, never betray your ability to inspire with well-rehearsed, quality delivery. Whether conveying information to an audience of 1 or 1,000, you need to make sure you feel good about your vocal delivery and that your visual delivery is strong, not awkward. You need to get a good feel for the timing and flow of your message. This is especially true, given that when you deliver content in the workplace, you are likely to be interrupted with feedback and questions.

Perfecting your delivery requires knowing how you need to come across and rehearsing until you nail it. Rehearsing your delivery and imagining the various rebuttals or interruptions will give you a feel for how to pivot back to your message seamlessly, without appearing flustered. Additionally, quality rehearsal will help you to catch gaps in your logic and discover ways to strengthen the content of your message.

THE LINK BETWEEN CONFIDENCE AND COMPETENCE

If you are like most of my clients, you want people in your workplace to believe that you are competent, capable, and credible. But unless you are subject to frequent standardized testing, chances are that your competence is something perceived, not proven. The way that people will perceive your competence is a by-product not only of the actual content you communicate, but also (and often more so) by how you deliver that content. So, if the goal is to be perceived as competent, it's not enough to be smart; you must prepare compelling messages *and* deliver them effectively.

When asked to deliver a message, remember there is a reason why you were chosen. Think of the last time you were asked to draft and send a memo or prepare and deliver a status update. What was the reason? Of course, it is possible that you got stuck doing someone else's work, but the more likely answer is that you are the expert on that topic. I've never been to a meeting where the least-informed person spoke to a team of experts. Nor have I known of a situation where a miserably uninformed person was responsible for drafting and sending a critical memo to people who already knew it all. If you are chosen to deliver the message to a team of 2 or a room of 200, it is most likely because you are the dedicated expert sharing a message to people who know less, and perhaps even care less, about the topic.

Given that your audience likely knows less about the topic than you do, what is the most logical way for the audience to discern your credibility and competence? The answer: your confidence. Don't believe me? Watch the news or a live sporting event. Check out a political debate. Who is winning on-air: someone who speaks with the accuracy of an encyclopedia but seems to have shaky and underdeveloped confidence, or someone who has unflappable confidence, and from the best you can tell, appears to know what he or she is talking about? Most of the time we may not even know the people talking on TV, yet we somehow manage to make assumptions about them, and whether we like listening to them and what they are saying.

Jaime just left a lucrative investment bank job, where he focused on real estate deals, to run global real estate in-house for a major tech firm. He has been in his new role for an entire week, and he is now expected to deliver a boardroom presentation in his second week on the job to a few senior leaders. His goal is to convince them that the plans in place for the next fiscal year and foreseeable future are solid. The guy is ridiculously smart, but he was visibly shaking when talking with me about the small-group presentation he is soon to give. After a bit of processing, he was able to articulate what was shaking his confidence and shared, "In my previous job, I felt so confident because people knew me already and they trusted me. These people don't know me yet, so if I mess up on this presentation, that will be their only impression of me." And he is not wrong. Some of the principles that I used with Jaime are important for us to consider here.

We know people are persuaded by individuals who demonstrate credibility. When it comes to the content of your message, you can incorporate credibility by referencing your experience. You can lean on credibility from outside sources (such as a reputable study or example). You can also establish credibility by demonstrating how a topic is relevant to your audience, which demonstrates shared values between you and them. While the principles of credibility and highlighting shared values are always important, they are especially critical when seeking to establish connection with people outside your core team, like cross-functional partners and external stakeholders.

In terms of delivery, however, you will be perceived as credible when you speak authentically and confidently. And it is important that you do so because we know audiences are more likely to stay focused on the content, and are even more likely to be persuaded, if they believe the speaker stands behind the message. I intentionally combine these words "authentically and confidently" because it is imperative that in today's market you demonstrate both and with apparent ease. In the story I shared earlier about the failed founder, had he done proper communication training and preparation, he would have discovered ways to demonstrate authentic leadership *and* confidence, which would have been a winning combination.

Portraying confidence (which is not the same as cockiness!) is critical to being an effective communicator in the workplace. I frequently coach people on how to demonstrate confidence in their everyday interactions—meetings, client calls, and so on. To do this (and I recommend you try this with a trusted friend or colleague), I role-play as the CEO, board member, client, or manager, and I ask my client to give his or her position on an important topic being managed at work. Or I role-play as an interviewer and have my client talk through his or her work experience with me. The purpose of these activities is to help people discover and nurture their most authentically confident communication style. The goal is not to hold yourself to a gold standard of confidence, but to help draw out your most natural, likable, confident style.

When doing this, be sure to listen and look for confidence betrayers, such as weak phrases or negative visual and vocal cues. Notice when you make throwaway phrases like, "Well, this seems kind of important because it was talked about" or "This seems like something we maybe should consider." Admittedly, all of us are prone to speaking some worthless phrases when thinking about what to say or hedging our bets, but we should work toward reducing them as much as possible.

As well, there are numerous visual and vocal behaviors that betray confidence. Nervous and involuntary movements, darting eyes, too many filler words, and unnecessary vocal upticks are signals to others that you may be either insecure or unenthusiastic about what you are saying. When you use tentative or vague language, or your visual and vocal delivery skills look and sound timid, people are more likely to question your credibility or the authenticity of what you're saying. Thus, it is imperative that you are sharp both in what you say and how you say it.

DO WHAT CONFIDENT COMMUNICATORS DO

With regard to oral communication (the words you speak) and decisions related to message content, confident communicators use assuring and descriptive language. But even more than this, confident communicators are intentional with their nonverbal behavior. If your goal is to instill confidence, be sure to practice incorporating erect posture, purposeful movements, open gestures, and strong eye contact in every workplace interaction. Yes, even virtual calls!

Strengthen Your Vocal Delivery

Erect posture will also help your vocal quality, giving you a stronger voice with more volume. If your voice is still shaky when speaking in meetings, don't start looking away from people; instead, find the friendliest face in the group and imagine that you two are simply having coffee together.

Your vocal delivery consists of many things; some may seem common knowledge and others not so much. When you talk, the person listening to you is evaluating how articulate you are; your voice's pitch, rate, timbre, tone, and emotion; and your use of filler words and pauses. People may not know they are doing it, but most likely they are forming an overall perception of you based on each of these vocal qualities.

Each time you speak, others are evaluating your articulation. (Sub)consciously they may be thinking something like, *She speaks really clearly. I like that I can understand her very easily.* An important distinction here is that many of my clients who have English as their second language will often ask me, "How is my accent?" I usually smile and ask, "How is mine?" I playfully then ask, "Would you like to hear me speak in your first language? Because I can't! I know one language, and I, like you, am still trying to improve my English every day!"

All of us have an accent. None is better than the other. Certainly, there are regions and markets that gravitate toward certain vocal stylings, and these tend to be represented in your local news channels. But even if there were a most popular accent in the world, what would it matter if it were delivered without confidence? So, if people wish to modify their accents, that is their choice, but no matter your accent, and no matter how fast or fluent your language skills, all of us have a better chance of accomplishing our communication goals when we articulate our messages with all the confidence we can muster.

By practicing some of the communication essentials here, you will minimize the risk of being perceived as unconfident or even inarticulate while increasing the likelihood of attaining your goal as a communicator.

Reduce Filler Words—and Try Not to Use Them at All!

Many people comment to me that—umm, like, you know—they wish they could stop saying filler words (aka verbal disfluencies). Vocal fillers are sounds and words that fill silence and do not add to the content of a message (e.g., "uh," "um," "like," etc.). Using these filler words

will hinder the clarity of your message because they're distracting to whomever you are speaking to.

For example, I know interviewers who will completely dismiss job candidates who use too many filler words. They'll tell me something like, "I really liked him. He's a smart guy. But if he talks like that in an interview, I can't put him in front of senior leadership or a client." This is because vocal fillers influence the perceptions of your credibility, preparedness, and confidence. If you speak with too many fillers, people will likely perceive you as unprepared, not credible, and insecure. When you speak inarticulately and use excessive filler words, you not only betray your message, but you are also causing people to work too hard to understand you. And, if people have to work hard to understand you, they may be prone to tune you out in favor of daydreaming or multitasking.

While some of my clients come to me hoping to completely eliminate all filler words, I remind them that this may not be the best goal. Truth is, unless you are giving a State of the Union type of presentation, most people expect an occasional filler word. Used sparingly and effectively, they can make you more relatable to your audience, give you time to catch your breath, and emphasize key points. But when they become crutch words used out of nervousness or lack of preparation, they diminish your credibility.

If you recognize a word you overuse, such as "like" or starting sentences with "you know," you can begin training yourself to reduce your use. I had a friend who wore a rubber band on his wrist and would snap it every time he used a filler word. It worked for him. But I'd like to think we can discover a less painful way to break vocal habits. I find one of the best ways to eliminate fillers is to slow your rate of speech and master the art of the pause.

Master the Pause

Many communicators struggle to embrace the pause. This is probably because even the briefest pause can feel like forever. But it usually only feels that way to you, the speaker, the one in the hot seat. Like filler words, pauses give you a chance to take a break and figure out what you want to say next. When used effectively, a pause has the added benefit of making you appear confident and in control, whereas overused filler words are distracting and make you sound as if you don't know what to say. A well-timed pause may also play to the emotion in the room, as it causes people to sit with a thought and reflect on what has been said or what they anticipate hearing next. Pausing allows you to collect your thoughts and get back on track. A strategically placed silence can build suspense, emphasize a point, or give your listener time to absorb a key insight.

Pausing gives you a moment to breathe and reengage with whomever you're speaking to. If you demonstrate assuredness—through erect posture and strong eye contact—as you pause, people are likely to give you the benefit of the doubt and determine that your pause is intentional. I encourage you to build pauses into your messages, letting them feel like an organic part of the way you talk.

Set the Tone and Emotion

An engaging vocal delivery helps you connect with your audience and can be used to highlight key concepts. Your tone and emotion do more than just captivate the people you're talking to; they also increase the likelihood a message will be remembered fondly. They strengthen the likelihood that your message will be remembered at all.

If you care about your message and you want the other person (i.e., your audience) to also care, then at minimum, increase your tone and emotion, as it will drive the likelihood that people will remember, perhaps ruminate on, what you shared. Although you can, of course, inject your voice with exaggerated tone and emotion when the moment calls for it, your default mode should be to speak with a warm and inviting voice, as though you have just opened the doors of your home to friends and neighbors.

Following the metaphor, just as you'd guide first-time visitors on a warm and inviting tour of your home, so too you would guide your audience with a warm, inviting, and conversational tone from the start through the finish of your message. Warm tone and emotion increase the likelihood that people will relate to you, and people tend to like others they can relate with.

Match Your Content with Your Vocal and Visual Delivery

Vocal (e.g., pausing) and visual (e.g., eye contact) elements of delivery work better together. A pause with strong eye contact and erect posture conveys a different meaning than a pause with someone slouched and staring at the table. Even more, your vocal and visual delivery works best when it matches the words you are speaking. People who are giddy to see a loved one may raise the pitch of their voices and throw open their arms as they say, "I've missed you! Get over here and give me a hug!" You can imagine how weird it would be to hear someone say those words with a high-pitched voice but a body that is slouched and closed off.

One of the biggest dilemmas people seem to face is what to do with their hands. This isn't only a stage problem, either. Some people release their nerves during high-stakes meetings or job interviews by gesturing awkwardly with their hands. If you find yourself on virtual calls or meetings fidgeting with your pen or making unnatural gestures while speaking, get a tennis ball and casually play with it in your lap. Most of my clients don't believe me until they try it. It is silent, it will allow you to release nerves, and no one will be the wiser.

There are also unusual occasions where you must really make sure your visual delivery is thoughtful, or perhaps even choreographed. For example, I've worked with financial leaders preparing earnings reports, and when we begin rehearsing a presentation intended to calm the audience with words like "all in all, things are looking up" or "profits are on the rise," they often push their hands in a downward motion as they say it. Here is where a quality rehearsal and being mindful of all the details of your delivery can make the difference, especially when we know people pay more attention to what you do than what you say.

Thus whether communicating in person or virtually, ensure your vocal and visual deliveries are coordinated with and enhancing your message, never betraying it!

MAKE EYE CONTACT

Eye contact is mission critical for effective communication in the workplace. Yes, of course it's important for demonstrating confidence and exuding executive presence, but it's more than that. It's actually critical to memory and retention, especially during conversations and virtual meetings,[1] where any number of additional distractions may be present. So, whether you are trying to ensure you remember what the other person is saying or you are hoping to increase the likelihood that someone else will remember what you are saying, it is important that your eye-contact game is strong.

There are some quick tips to remember when trying to increase your eye contact. For starters, a good rule of thumb is to try to make eye contact 50 to 70 percent of the time during conversation. Of course, you don't want to stare at someone's eyes for minutes at a time. It's actually normal to look into another's eyes for roughly five seconds before glancing away momentarily. If you are like many people I work with, this may seem impossible to do, especially when you are the one speaking.

If you feel like you have room to grow when it comes to good eye contact, you aren't alone. Kids are growing up with devices in hand. They also are observing their own parents glued to their phones. My heart breaks when I see a kid holler something like, "Dad, watch me do this cannonball!" and I see the dad make a thumbs-up and respond, "Great job!"—all while staring at his phone. I'm not innocent either. During family dinner, my pocket buzzes and I feel that urge to check my phone while remaining part of the conversation. Not only are adults trading eye contact for screen time, but our poor behavior-modeling is teaching young people that eye contact is unimportant.

The struggle is real, and many individuals I work with need help strengthening their eye contact. Yet when I suggest doing eye-contact drills with my clients, some will look at me as though I've asked them to write a sentence in cursive script. *Write the sentence . . . why wouldn't I just type it? Write it in cursive . . . who even does that anymore?* I fear that eye contact, like cursive writing, is on the brink of becoming a lost art. The rarer it becomes, the more precious it will become. Those who do it well will continue to be seen as those leaders among us who have the "it" factor; a certain magnetism we crave and almost miss. This is because somewhere inside of us we know how good it feels to be seen and how much we appreciate eye contact that is warm, inviting, and kind, and that displays confidence and sincerity.

Plenty has been written about the cultural cues to be mindful of when considering giving and receiving eye contact. Most agree that Western culture places a premium on eye contact, with perception being that people who give too little eye contact are either impolite, insecure, or perhaps even untrustworthy. While staring or giving creepy eye contact is intimidating and awkward—and may even appear threatening—appropriately strong eye contact leads us to like a person more (and interestingly, research shows that it may even lead us to find them more attractive).[2]

The expectations for eye contact during one-on-one conversation remain mostly true for presentations to small and large groups. No matter the environment, you would be wise to give great eye contact, even when not receiving it, and hope that by modeling it well, others may reciprocate in kind.

When it comes to presenting, savvy speakers aim to make eye contact with each person in the room, and many will work the room with their eyes by going from one side to the other or making natural z-type patterns with their eyes. That said, it would be unnatural and very awkward to meet eyes with each person down the row, handing each person a moment of eye contact like you were passing out candy.

Solid eye contact need not be longer than five seconds without breaking. Even in one-to-one interaction, eye contact may only last the duration of a phrase or thought. One of the biggest perks of great eye contact is that you can keep a continuous gauge of how others in the room are receiving your message, allowing you to adjust your content or delivery in real time.

The good news is that growing your eye contact skills is simple. Think of eye contact like a muscle. If you grow it, it will be there and ready for you when you need it. If you don't grow it, you can't expect to have it for use. Imagine spending your life without ever lifting a thing and then walking into the gym and reaching for the 100-pound dumbbells, expecting to rep heavy weight. Not going to happen.

But the person who goes to the gym and reps the lighter weights will see progress in time. With a commitment to lifting, that person will soon be reaching for heavier and heavier weights, and before long, growing the muscles needed for lifting those heavy weights.

Your eye contact muscles work similarly. And eye contact during high-stake interactions is heavy weight, intended for those with strong eye contact muscles. So, if you are prone to avoiding and ignoring eye contact with others and tend to spend your days staring at devices, attempting to have a meaningful interaction, engage in a difficult conversation, or deliver a presentation may seem exhausting, if not impossible. Start by treating each human interaction as a chance to grow eye contact muscles. Wave, smile, and make eye contact with the person crossing the street. Make eye contact and say a friendly hello to the person passing you in the grocery store. Make small talk using strong eye contact with your barista next time you order a coffee. If you practice eye contact in low-stake interactions, your muscles will grow and be readily available in time for the high-stake interactions. If 60 seconds of eye contact with the barista seems uncomfortable, how can you expect to maintain eye contact throughout a 45-minute job interview or 20-minute presentation, when the stakes are much higher for your success?

DON'T BE DISMAYED BY "NETFLIX FACE"

One of the reasons that people struggle to have strong eye contact and otherwise effective delivery is because they perceive that other people are disinterested. My clients tell me it's really difficult to run a meeting or give a presentation to a room of seemingly disengaged others, and even harder when it's a virtual call and half or more screens are off.

As an example, one of my clients, Georgia, dedicated a large amount of her time working with me to prepare for an important presentation she was going to deliver to the team she managed. After it was over, she told me that she felt she had nailed the presentation, delivering her ideas with passion and confidence, but that to her dismay, her team members seemed to be bored to death during her presentation. The odd part was that many of her team members came to her later, applauding the great job she had done and saying that they fully supported her ideas.

My explanation for this is what I call "Netflix face." Years ago, we were entertained in groups. We went to movie houses with friends, sat near strangers, and shared a collective laugh out loud. During the week, we snacked in the living room, watching sitcoms with family. Now, we stream content on our devices with earbuds, which I believe has led to a new skill for having muted responses to mediated content. Perhaps it is because laughing alone seems awkward. Certainly, when others around us are laughing, we feel freer to laugh louder. But I think muted responses might be due also to our desire to not draw attention or disturb others. Children are handed devices with headphones and told to be quiet. Adults likewise consume media individually while in communal spaces, so now it seems impolite to laugh out loud when something is funny or to begin crying in public. We are daily training ourselves to consume media and entertainment in isolation. And I believe this new skill carries its way into meetings and other workplace environments.

But whether it is "Netflix face" or some other cause, at the end of the day, you as a communicator have a goal, and it is your job to project the energy that you wish to receive. One of my best friends writes music and performs regularly. Early in his career, when playing at coffee shops of 20 people sipping lattes and only partly listening to him and his band, I asked how he gets himself to play his heart out when people are hardly listening. He admitted that it was hard and that there are occasions where a member of the band will start to lower his or her energy because of small crowd size or lack of audience involvement. But he reminded me that you can't do that. He likened it to a boomerang—you never get back what you don't first throw out there.

I am certainly not a stage musician, but I believe the same principle applies for you and me. As an academic, it's not uncommon for me to sit in meetings with grumpy faculty. But I can't merely reflect their energy and expect them to take interest in my message. Instead, I must *infuse* the room with new energy. In meetings, how are you using your vocal and visual delivery to energize others and warm them to your ideas? In your memos and emails, how are you framing the content to ensure that people are feeling your energy and excitement behind your ideas? There is not one right way to do this, but the critical takeaway here is that you can choose what kind of energy you put out into the world. You can't expect to receive a positive charge that you aren't willing to give first.

Be forewarned, however, that while you might in fact be nailing your team status update or client call, the faces around the room may not show it. When people don't perk up with big smiles, it's possible they are multitasking. They may be fully engaged but forget how to show it. You must remain calm and confident, and give it your best. In small or large meetings, look for the one or two people who will make eye contact and nod their heads. Let that positive feedback loop fill your soul and carry you forward. As you reward your head-nodders with smiles and eye contact, watch how quickly others will begin to participate in hopes of earning your favorable feedback as well.

YOU'VE GOT TO SELL IT

Ultimately, it's your job to have a great message and sell it. My family has a funny phrase for when people are making their case for something they want. We jokingly remind them, "Don't just say it, sell it." In other words, don't merely ask if we can have pizza tonight; instead, make a compelling case for why. Not long ago, we were returning from the park when Joy, my oldest, asked me to turn up a song on the radio. She started singing along quietly. We then pulled up to a streetlight, and the car beside us was a family we knew well. Joy said, "Turn it up, and put my window down." It was clear to me she wanted to go full-blown Carpool Karaoke for this one.

As I was putting the window down, her little sister, Evy, slapped her on the arm and said, "Don't just sing it, Joy! You've got to sell it!" Joy threw on some oversized sunglasses, grabbed the hairbrush-microphone from the seat pocket in front of her, and transformed herself into a mini Elton John. The passengers in the car beside us seemed to enjoy the show as much as we did because she didn't just sing the song. She sold it.

This is my challenge for you and me: When the moment matters, what are we doing or what should we be doing to appropriately sell the message? In writing memos, we are limited to our use of the words themselves. But in everyday interactions and when presenting our ideas in meetings or groups, we have an opportunity to do more than rely on the words themselves. We should be asking ourselves: *What do I want this person (or, these people) to think of me and my message? How do I want them to respond?* There is a whole world of vocal and visual delivery skills available to us, and we ought to master them as best as we are able. By doing so, we don't just sing the song. We sell it.

● ● ●

When it comes to delivering your messages with impact, the struggle is real. The message sent is not always the message received, and this problem is magnified because many people lack the willingness to own the message or the readiness to do so effectively. You can be different. You can do better.

With the right *mindset*, a willingness to try, learn, and grow, you can develop the readiness to be a best-in-class communicator. Developing *audience-centered messages* that are *clear, concise, and compelling* should be standard for every note you send and every time you speak. *Confident vocal and visual delivery* should become second nature for you.

ESSENTIAL TAKEAWAYS

- Gain credibility from the very start and throughout your entire message by simply demonstrating the vocal and visual delivery skills that project confidence.

- Try not to use filler words, such as "like," "you know," "umm," and "uh" since they distract listeners from the message you really want to get across.

- Pause occasionally when speaking, so you have more time to choose your words carefully and decide what you really want to say next.

- Make and maintain eye contact as much as possible.

- Think about what impression you make *before* you even speak.

Choose the Best MEDIUM for Your Message

Communication Star

Goal

Medium

Audience perception

Messenger

Message

"The medium *is* the message" is a familiar argument to communication scholars.[1] The simplest explanation being that the medium you choose to convey your message holds as much if not more meaning than the message itself. There is a lot to consider in regard to workplace communication and the mediums through which we communicate.

Don't get too hung up on the word "medium." Some people debate whether and when to use *medium* versus *channel* or some other term. And that is fine, but for our purposes, let's just think of a medium as the means by which people send and receive messages. For example, one of my clients is the CEO of a fintech startup, and he recently texted me, "Call me ASAP." I called and quickly realized he was driving home and furious with someone in his C suite as he fumed, "I'm firing him tonight, and I need to get the wording right. Can you help me draft an email while I drive?" I laughingly responded, "Yes, but no. . . . Yes, I can, but no I won't because it would be malpractice."

He seemed surprised by my response. As we talked it out, he ultimately agreed that an email sent in the heat of the night would have been all wrong. I hope he knew that already and was just looking to vent a little. He ended up firing the guy, but he did it the right way, not via email. When it was all over, I called him and said, "Just to be clear, if you ever ask, I will not be able to help you call off your wedding engagement via text message." He laughed, which hopefully meant that the lesson was learned: the medium matters.

Think back to times you may have learned you were hired into a role or perhaps even let go from a job. What medium was used, and how did that make you feel? Just like some people gush when sharing an engagement story (e.g., "he spelled out 'marry me' in rose petals") where it is clear that the medium carried additional meaning, messages in the workplace take on different meanings based on how they are conveyed. The words "Congrats, looks like you are getting promoted" will more often than not cause one to do a happy dance. That said, the same promotion message being delivered in person accompanied by a giant smile, high five, and nice bottle of champagne feels altogether different than if it was sent via internal messaging tool (sandwiched between other messages like "running late to call, will join soon" and "forward me that memo ASAP").

The medium may not be a deal breaker—chances are that you still celebrate the promotion—but consider the opportunity missed when we rely on only the most convenient medium for communication. In this case, the extra effort of choosing a richer medium like being in person or at least setting up a five-minute video call allows you to give additional value and meaning to the very message itself.

The word of advice here is that when something is going to be memorable, you must be especially intentional. "Can you send me that memo?" is not particularly memorable. That is the everyday way of getting things done. No need to meet in person and high five over such a message. "You are getting promoted," however, is a big deal, and will likely be a story told to friends and family. How do you want that story told? Do you want someone to say, "Look, here is the message from my manager, just after he asked me to send him the memo." Or do you want that story to go, "He stopped by my office unannounced, held up a bottle of champagne, and congratulated me!"

Savvy communicators know to choose their medium wisely, and this is especially true when a memory will be made that becomes a story retold.

SO MANY WAYS TO COMMUNICATE A MESSAGE

Think of how a single piece of information gets shared:

- A pediatrician texts (*medium*) his staff to say he won't make it to the office today.

- The staff immediately sends emails (*mediums*) and calls (*mediums*) everyone scheduled for that day to alert them that their children's appointments are cancelled.

- I receive the email (*medium*) and proceed to walk outside and tell (*medium*) my wife, who then calls (*medium*) the school to let the school staff know that our daughter will not be leaving early.

- The school staff delivers a handwritten note (*medium*) to the teacher who then walks up to my daughter to tell (*medium*) her the news.

- My daughter flashes a big smile across her face (*medium*) before saying (*medium*) "Yes! That means I can stay for recess and I don't have to get a shot today!"

In this example, one pediatrician missed work, and it resulted in the microcoordination of numerous messages that were conveyed through varying communication mediums. It's incredible that we live in a world with such capability to communicate with ease across varying mediums. Texting with friends across the globe. Hosting virtual happy hours. Livestreaming weddings and other celebrations for those unable to attend in person.

It is also incredible that with one click of a button, a single human can bypass traditional mediums and communicate directly with millions of people. The modern president doesn't have to depend on the press corps or designated public relations team to transmit or convey a message. To date, former President Barack Obama is the most followed Twitter account, with more than 130 million followers. Runner-up is Justin Bieber with more than 114 million followers. (I guess that means that if Bieber were your family pediatrician and he got sick today, many steps could be eliminated from the communication chain. He would tweet (*medium*), and then you and 114 million others would know that you need to call (*medium*) his office to reschedule your kid's appointment.)

WHAT TO CONSIDER WHEN CHOOSING WHICH MEDIUM TO USE

There are clear advantages to living in a society with so many rapid and far-reaching communication mediums. However, there are some liabilities to consider also. International leaders have lost their license to tweet. Celebrities have been defamed by inflammatory messages on social media. And bringing it home for everyday citizens, how often do you imagine people wish they had taken 30 more seconds to think through an email message before clicking send?

Indeed, there is much to weigh when considering the medium. There are times we choose the medium and others when it is chosen for us. There are times when we say no to communicating because the medium is not going to work. For example, when coronavirus erupted across the United States, most of my previously booked—*in person*—speaking engagements for the year fell apart. In some cases, the coordinator called me to cancel. In other cases, the show went on virtually because the presentation still made good sense and worked just as well virtually as it would have in person.

In some cases, however, I had to act on conscience and turn down good money by advising some clients to cancel or postpone events because a virtual version of the workshop would not have achieved the same learning outcomes nor would it have been in the best interest of the participants. It would have been easier for me—I didn't have to travel and I could conduct the workshop from my home office while wearing running shorts and drinking coffee brewed in my own kitchen—but I knew the goals would have been compromised and the quality of message and meaning for the intended audience diminished by the medium.

Notably, I have had several clients reflect on how much they appreciate the equalizing dimension of meeting and presenting in virtual environments. While I have yet to formally study this, feedback from clients and students suggests a few surprising finds about videoconferencing. Softer-spoken individuals and those who take up less physical space are appreciating what feels like a level playing field for interaction. In video calls, smaller and quieter people can turn down the volume of louder colleagues and visually see that their square on the screen takes up the same amount of space as their colleagues. Conversely, those individuals who communicate power with a commanding visual and vocal presence are finding it harder to hold the floor and dominate dialogue. This would explain why some of my clients who successfully command more floor in face-to-face environments feel they are missing something in virtual mediums, while others are surprised to find their voice and more sense of self while working remotely.

In other words, when selecting your medium, just like when making decisions on the message itself, you must be goal-oriented and audience-centered. The medium you choose is an extension of you and your message. If you ever said or heard "I hate to do this over the phone, but . . . ," you or the other person recognized that the medium was not best for the situation, but did so anyway and tried to right the wrong by some acknowledgment or apology. Or what about when you call someone and there is no answer, but then five seconds later you receive a text like, "Missed your call, what's up?" Possibly the person is in a meeting and can't answer. It is also possible the person wants to communicate with you but not via your chosen medium. Instead, the sender wants to communicate via his or her chosen medium—texting.

I hear from clients all the time that their manager will regularly cancel weekly meetings by saying something like, "Hey, I am slammed this week. Let's cancel our one-on-one. Send me any updates/questions you have for me." I bet if you are like my clients, you won't read into that the first time. You might even appreciate getting back the time that you had allocated to that meeting.

By the second or third time this happens, though, you might notice two things. First is the message of power: your manager is exercising the power to cancel meetings with you, and the (not so) subtle message being received is that you are not worthy of your boss's time. With 24 hours in a day, your boss has time but not for you. The second realization is that your communication medium with your manager has been relegated to asynchronous messaging, rather than what you had anticipated, which is synchronous interactions virtually or face-to-face. Depending on the desired relationship with your manager, this might be a total bummer or welcome news. Either way, however, it's a message with meaning that illuminates and conveys more than the sender likely ever intended.

Whether corporate budget dollars or individuals considering everyday opportunity cost, communicators are regularly weighing the medium. Marketers long weighed the cost and benefits of running a newspaper ad, billboard campaign, radio spot, or television commercial. Companies and influencers are still discovering to what extent they should rely on social media marketing as the medium for distributing their message. Weighing the cost and benefit of various communication mediums is not just a decision companies make.

Like a company with only so much budget, you only have so much time in a day. If you are like most people, you (sub)consciously make numerous decisions each day about how to manage your communication. Instinctively you are making decisions about your economy of time and the opportunity cost of communication when interacting.

Consider a scenario where your colleague sends you a note requesting time to connect. Do you book a lunch meeting or make a five-minute call on your drive home? If you choose to get lunch with your colleague, do you give your undivided attention, or do you respond to notifications on your phone every so often? If so, the phone has become an extension of you like a medium that is now impacting, if not completely impeding, the interaction. The lunch meeting is no longer an exclusive, intimate, face-to-face interaction. Your friend is now receiving a clear message that you are as (if not more) interested in and engaged with a screen the size of a hand, as you are with him or her.

If the medium is the message, what messages are you sending given the mediums you use and how you use them? Star communicators are goal-oriented and audience-centered. They don't merely develop sharp content and deliver it effectively. They are careful in choosing the medium.

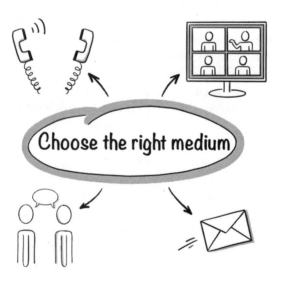

Choose the right medium

MAKE TIME TO COMMUNICATE ABOUT YOUR COMMUNICATION

One of your first action items when joining a team, getting a new manager, or leading a group is to get very clear about when and how to communicate with one another. I could share story after story about clients telling me their work frustrations, and far too many examples would point back to avoidable communication woes. The boss who messages at night and on the weekend. The manager who expects face-to-face meetings to be a tech-free zone, to the shock and dismay of her reports. The colleagues who send too many non-work-related messages on channels dedicated for business. The person who joins meetings but never turns on video. People who fail to monitor the Slack channel but are great via email and vice versa. These are just a few examples. For this reason, don't wait until frustration sets in to communicate about how to communicate. I am reminded of my client who shared that his performance evaluation went great, except for one irritating comment apparently left by his manager that went something like, "He needs to stop emailing so many attachments to calendar invites. The files are too large, people don't know to read them, and it is frustrating to receive. He should post them to the channel, where they belong." My client was really shaken up while reading this to me, because he felt unfairly attacked by an expectation that had never been told to him, and even more, it seemed so insignificant.

But it makes the point that people develop expectations about communication mediums. My client had come from a previous job where attaching related documents to a calendar invite was standard operating procedure; in fact, it was a considerate thing to do. Unbeknownst to him, his manager at his new job frowned on that, and somehow expected that my client would automatically know that such a thing was wrong to do. And rather than take two minutes to educate him about the matter, the manager decided to blast him in the evaluation. I hope you will learn from his lesson.

When you are new to an organization, it is likely that people will give you the rundown of what communication tools people use and how. It is also very important that you take the initiative to ask people, especially those you report to, very early on about their own communication style and preference. You could start by asking your manager questions like:

- "What is your preferred way for sending and receiving information? For instance, what kind of situations would you rather I meet with you versus message you?"

- "When sending you updates, do you prefer one larger message with updates about numerous topics, or do you prefer that I send you separate messages by topic?"

- "What about communicating after business hours? I want to be sure that I am communicating in a timely manner but also respecting your time and work boundaries."

- "What kind of situation would it be important for me to contact you after your working hours, and how would you prefer that I reach you?" (Asking this question also allows an opportunity for you to share your own preferences and boundaries around when and how to be contacted after hours.)

The conversation about when and how to communicate best will be an ongoing one, but questions like these will help you get started down the right path. Likewise, you should be prepared to share your own communication styles, preferences, and expectations with people reporting to you or with any teams you lead.

As an example, I tell people who work with me that they are welcome to text my personal phone whenever they'd like, but to not hold any expectations around if or when I'll reply. I leave my phone in "do not disturb" mode most of the day, and so my messages get buried. If someone is giving me an action item or expecting that I remember to respond to a message, the best way is to email me. My communication preferences aren't right or wrong, but it would be wrong of me to hold others to communication expectations that I don't articulate. The lesson being that individuals develop certain preferences and expectations about when and how people communicate, and communicating about them sooner rather than later is essential.

WHAT'S NEXT

Part II opened by underscoring the importance of demonstrating a willingness to communicate and improve as a communicator. You can't run without first committing to lace up and go outside. We then walked through the points of how to become a star communicator: identify your communication goal, know what your audience wants, own your message, anticipate how your audience perceives you, and choose the appropriate medium for your message. Next, Part III dives deep into coaching tips for how to increase your communicator effectiveness in several specific situations—from job hunting to climbing the career ladder and more.

ESSENTIAL TAKEAWAYS

- The medium you choose to convey your message holds as much, if not more, weight than the message itself.

- When selecting which type of communication medium to use, you must be goal-oriented and audience-centered. The medium you choose is an extension of you and your message.

- You are (sub)consciously making decisions as a communicator, such as which medium will cost you the least time and effort while achieving your desired outcome.

- One of your first action items when joining a team, getting a new manager, or leading a group is to get very clear about when and how to communicate with one another.

PART III

BEYOND THE ESSENTIALS

Communicate Your Way into a Job

So far, this book has focused on knowing, understanding, and applying communication essentials, but this chapter takes a deep dive into how you can communicate effectively in order to get the job you want. More specifically, we will explore how to employ communication essentials when networking, applying, and interviewing.

As a first order of business, consider that communication is both *representational* (i.e., just the facts) and *presentational* (i.e., providing purposeful perspective about those facts). Representational communication says, "just the facts, ma'am." But presentational communication argues that "facts don't speak for themselves."

Many job seekers who fail at the application or interview stage may actually be representing themselves well (by conveying accurate facts), but are failing because they don't present themselves effectively. To win your dream job, you must *present* yourself, in a way that doesn't just "represent" the facts of who you are and what you've done, but actually motivates others to vouch for you, sponsor you, and hire you.

Importantly, you must be both an ethical communicator who does not misrepresent the facts *and* a persuasive communicator who presents yourself in a way that enables you to accomplish your career goals. Our word choices and nonverbal cues as well as how we frame and filter information are all examples of presentational communication at play. Scroll through your social media feed for a plethora of examples. While a 24-hour surveillance camera would be *representational* of my life and give you the play-by-play of my day without any editing, social media uploads are presentational and highlight the facts of my day as I want you to see and interpret them.

Just like social media uploads are a chosen presentation of self, it is expected that job candidates are wisely choosing how to present themselves on paper and in person. When a hiring manager says, "Walk me through your résumé," I certainly hope you don't blandly *represent* each fact of your work history. A savvy communicator recognizes this as the opportunity to present résumé details in a light most favorable for the goal of getting the job. Same is true of your actual résumé. Did you prepare that résumé to be an unbiased representation of your actual experiences at work and beyond? Or, did you emphasize those details that present your professional history in a way that will capture the reviewer's attention?

For example, consider a first-round interview with a hiring manager who is inquiring about your job history. Candidate A offers an honest representation of the facts as he remembers them: "Yeah, so, after coming out of college, I was finally able to land a job with . . ." Candidate B offers those same facts but provides a more inspiring presentation of them: "Gladly. Coming out of college, I was recruited into an exciting role with a team . . ." Remember, nothing about the facts has changed per se, but the presentation of those facts in just those five seconds has shaped the message.

To be clear, I do not endorse unethical representation of facts. I am endorsing that people represent themselves with honesty and integrity while simultaneously presenting themselves in a way that helps with goal attainment. A person on a date can be authentic *and* charming all at once. Someone leading a meeting can deliver information ethically *and* persuasively. So too can a person networking and interviewing for a job.

WORK YOUR NETWORK

I have clients who contact me and say their job searches are going nowhere. They've dropped more than 100 résumés and contacted dozens of people, but gotten zero bites. I ask them what steps they've taken, and they boast about upgrading their LinkedIn account, searching the site for jobs, and then messaging people (whom they've never met or been introduced to) who work at those companies. When I ask to see an example message that they are sending these unknown others, they show me what appears to be something between a talk track for a sales call and a full-blown cover letter. Please note that I don't know a single person who replies to those messages—because they come across like a phishing scam. It's possible that some lonely reader will find the message and think, *Hey, a new friend*, but chances are that person doesn't have a job lead for you.

If you called to tell me you had only one working day to jump-start your job search, I would advise you to spend 30 minutes or so sipping coffee and dreaming about your career. Next, I'd encourage you to research some of your ideas online and get a sense of trends in the job market. I would then advise you to invest the remainder of your day contacting people in your network to inquire about any possible ideas or opportunities they know about and are willing to share with you. I'd urge you to be straightforward about the fact you are exploring new opportunities and turning to them for advice.

Please note my intentional use of the word "advice," as opposed to "help." Dr. John Daly of The University of Texas at Austin taught me many things during my time as his student, and this slight yet important distinction of the words we use is one of them. My attempt to sum up his brilliant lecture is: Whereas asking people for *help* may immediately feel like you are taxing their time and effort (like you've just asked them to help you unpack your U-Haul), asking for advice is to invite them to play the role of a wise sage. Given those options and when appropriate to do so, I prefer to ask for "advice" rather than "help." Your goal is to convert each interaction into a next step, by saying things like this:

> "Javier, thank you so much for your time today. I appreciate you chatting with me. Before we say goodbye, I'd really appreciate it if you would give me an action item—something you'd advise me to do or someone you'd encourage me to connect with."

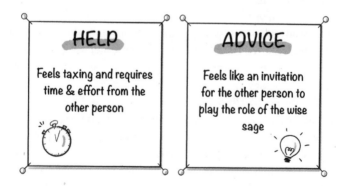

ESTABLISH AND MAINTAIN A ROBUST NETWORK

Of course, the challenge is that you can't work a network you don't have. For this reason, it is imperative to get in the habit of establishing and maintaining a robust network. A few years ago, an organization I presided over was hosting a gala. I had invited quite a crowd to attend, which included dignitaries and politicians. Two days after the event, I checked my mail and found a handwritten thank-you card from a well-known congressional leader. He had written to thank me for inviting him and his wife to join my table. He commented on the food, the event itself, and the enjoyable table conversations. He offered to buy me a meal next time we were in the same town. So I took him up on it.

The next month, while joining him for a breakfast taco at his favorite establishment, I inquired about the thank-you card. With genuine curiosity, I wanted to know if he actually wrote it—and if so, how he found time for such things, given the enormous demands on his time. With the kindest smile and twinkle in his eye, he shared that, in fact, he had written the letter. He then showed me his work bag, which included congressional work, a notepad, a newspaper, a very nice pen, and some stationery. He said that he made it a point throughout the day, but mostly in the morning over breakfast, to handwrite notes to a select few individuals he had encountered the day before. As he saw it, this daily habit took very little time, and in exchange, it kept his mind in a state of gratitude and with a focus on other people. As I saw it, he was also establishing a routine for surprising and delighting others around him.

You might not choose to carry stationery with you wherever you go, but I bet you have a smartphone with some pretty handy applications. Try this:

1. Start a new notebook on your phone where you can log information from your daily interactions.

2. Each time someone you'd like to stay connected with shares something with you that seems important to him or her, quickly jot it down in your new notebook (ideally, without the other person knowing you are doing so).

3. Every 48 to 72 hours, check your notes and do something with them. If you don't have anything in your notes, you need to start interacting with more people and do more listening. If you do have items in your notes, decide on a simple and smart action for how to support and encourage the people on your list.

Let me give you an example of how this works. On Monday, your colleague Fernando mentions to you that he can't make the meeting tomorrow because he is attending a GMAT prep course. You could let that piece of information go, or you could inquire about the course. By inquiring, you learn that he is eager to go back to school and get his MBA, but he is a bit nervous about the GMAT, which is why he enrolled in this GMAT prep course that meets every other Tuesday afternoon. *Aha!* You now have a piece of information to add to your notebook.

When checking your notebook two days later, you decide that a simple and smart action for how to support and encourage Fernando is to set a reminder in your phone for every other Tuesday to send a quick one-liner of encouragement to Fernando. Over the next three months, you send him a total of six encouraging text messages (e.g., *Happy GMAT Tuesday! Proud of you for pursuing your dreams!*).

In the example of Fernando, the cost is nominal. It's just six text messages that you didn't even have to remember. The calendar reminder did all the work. But the impact is huge. You have become a bit of surprise and delight to Fernando at a time when he needs it most. And, as a side note, the Fernando reminders simultaneously encouraged you to be less self-absorbed and more aware of others and their needs.

Now, multiply this habit by all the interactions in your life. By actively listening to others to understand their needs and looking for simple ways to cheer people on, you are becoming a happier and healthier person. You are becoming the kind of individual others want to know and network with. This fun and easy habit not only strengthens your interpersonal relationships, but it builds your empathy. The truth is building and maintaining healthy social and professional networks happens to be far better for you than you may realize. That your networks help you climb the ladder professionally is really just a bonus.

But without strong networks, climbing a professional ladder is nearly impossible. When it comes to job seeking, a mostly generic and lengthy note on LinkedIn outlining your skills and qualifications sent to dozens of people who don't know you and have zero reason to talk to you is far less promising than one phone call to someone who already knows you and likes you. Your quality contacts have a reason to support and sponsor your job search. They might have no ability to hire you, but they likely know someone who does, and that e-introduction is worth far more than a cold call or shotgun email. For these reasons, I urge all my clients to avoid spinning their wheels unnecessarily and to instead establish, maintain, and then work their networks.

WRITE YOUR WAY INTO AN INTERVIEW

In addition to gaining quality leads, scheduling calls, and booking some coffee chats, it's imperative that job seekers develop smart written application materials. While I have never known someone to get a job solely because of a cover letter and résumé, I have known many people to be extended interviews because their cover letters and résumés put them through to the interview phase. This is important to consider. If communication is about goal attainment, do your résumé and cover letter scream "give me any job" or are they written to motivate a specific person and organization to give you an interview? If you like wasting paper, write a generic brag reel and send it to every company with an opening.

Winning applicants realize that a cover letter is not the medium to toot your horn, prove your worth, or put readers to sleep by listing generic accomplishments. Instead, a cover letter is a chance to connect with your readers, declare clear interests in a specific career opportunity, and help a reader connect the dots between your qualifications, career goals, and the opportunity you are seeking. One solid cover letter written to apply for a specific position is better than a generic letter submitted to a hundred job postings with just the company name swapped.

A human or machine will try to make sense of your résumé in seconds. So while it may not always require the same level of exactness for the position and reader, it should always highlight the right experiences and credentials in a clear, concise, and compelling manner. It should also emphasize verbiage found on the job description. For example, if your current employer has labeled you and your colleagues a "core group," but the job you are seeking is looking for someone who has experience being part of a "high-performing team," it would be worth the two seconds to amend your résumé to make sure you are describing your experience using the language of your potential employer. There is no pride to be won in sticking to your terminology when you know your future employer uses different terms. If your boss offered you a seat on a sofa, would you correct your boss and call it a couch? I doubt it. My guess is that you will refer to the couch as a sofa— at least when your boss is around.

The essential takeaway here is to not get attached to your own way of describing information. Instead, learn and incorporate the language and jargon of your future employer, throughout your application materials and interviews. This is especially true in an era when artificial intelligence software is reading more résumés than humans.

INTERVIEW YOUR WAY INTO A JOB

There are any number of possible interview questions that a job candidate may be asked. For those who do not wish to memorize hundreds of answers to possible questions, I recommend a more viable preparation plan. Start with the basics. In most cases, an interviewer will spend the first part of the interview trying to gain a better understanding about who you are and why you want this opportunity. So, to make a good first impression, it's important to nail these.

The "who are you" prompt will often be the first real interview question and is usually posed like this: "Walk me through your résumé" or "Tell me about yourself" or "What's your story?" One trick is gauging time and tone. For a simple rule of thumb, walking someone through your résumé can take up to two minutes, whereas telling someone about yourself should be done in about one minute. As for tone, given that this is usually the opening to an interview, it's important to establish your core messaging during this exchange. If I were interviewing for a job, I would want the interviewer to know that I am a grateful and humble human who is capable and confident in my abilities, and mostly that I am excited to be interviewing for this job and would be eager to drive value in the position. So while I might be walking the interviewer through my résumé, my core messaging must convey gratitude, humility, capability, confidence, excitement, and eagerness.

Thus, if I were being interviewed as a possible candidate for writing this book, and if I were asked at the start of the interview, "Walk me through your résumé," I might say:

> "Cheryl, first, thank you so much for making time to visit with me. The opportunity to write a book for McGraw Hill would be an absolute thrill, and I am so grateful to be considered.
>
> "I'd love to walk you through my résumé, and I believe you will find that my background, education, and experiences have prepared me well for this role. Likewise, this opportunity is directly aligned with my career goals. So, all together, it's an ideal fit.
>
> "I grew up in Texas and studied communication as an undergraduate student. I was fortunate to have faculty and mentors who invested time in me. They modeled for me what it means to be a best-in-class academic and overall good person.
>
> "Their belief in me gave me the confidence to go on and earn a doctorate in communication. And while doing so, I had the incredible privilege of rapid learning and professional growth. You could say I was drinking water from a firehose. I took doctoral courses, gained research experience, served as a teaching and research assistant, and simultaneously launched my own research projects and picked up teaching positions at nearby colleges. To top it off, I was invited by leaders at our business school to begin facilitating executive education workshops and communication coaching for MBA students.

"All of that was more than a decade ago. And since that time, I have remained a dedicated student of human communication and continue to refine my approach when teaching the communication essentials to students, clients, and people of all ages and various walks of life. I've joyfully given hundreds of lectures and talks on communication, and I've personally coached over a thousand individuals. Learning about and teaching communication is extremely life-giving for me.

"For these reasons and many others, I am so thrilled for the possibility to publish this book with you. Again, thank you so much for your time. I am very grateful for the opportunity to talk with you today."

Remember that a "walk me through your résumé" or "tell me about yourself" response should be music to their ears and leave them wanting more. It usually is the beginning of a conversation and should be a high-level overview to assure them you are ready for the opportunity and that you have the attitude of someone they will enjoy working with. Per my example, a smart "walk me through your résumé" should bookend with an attitude of gratitude and eagerness. It has a clear, linear story focused on how my background, education, experiences, and career goals align with the opportunity I seek.

Some may read the example and say, "That doesn't tell them enough specifics." In some circumstances, it may benefit you to subtly name-drop appropriate people, places, and things, as well as reference specific achievements or stats that are appropriate for the opportunity being sought, but only if you can do so without sounding like a braggart or getting too deep into the weeds of your background.

If you end the right way, as in my example, your interviewer's most natural response will be: "Thank you for sharing, and likewise, we are grateful to be visiting with you. Tell me a little more about why you are seeking this particular opportunity." Or, they might say, "Why do you want to work here?" or "Why this industry?" or "Why our company?" In other words, after getting a feel for you and hearing your story, most interviewers want to know why you want to be part of their team and what they are doing.

The mistake I see most people make when answering the "why us" question (e.g., why this industry, this role, or this company) is they overemphasize themselves and their prior experience rather than focusing on the new opportunity. Imagine you are on a first date and the person across the table asks why you want to go out with them. Would you talk about yourself and your past dating relationships? Would you focus on what's in it for you? No! I certainly hope not. You should focus on your date. As a general rule of thumb, I encourage clients to develop a full-bodied response to whatever "why us" question they receive.

For example, suppose you are interviewing for a role as a technology consultant with a top firm and I ask, "What do you find appealing about this particular opportunity?" I'd advise you to answer in some way similar to this:

> (Intro) "Trey, I appreciate you allowing me a chance to share a bit about my interest in this opportunity. I see myself at a crossroads in my career. I've had great experiences thus far, each of which has helped me to discover more of myself and where I thrive best. And because of that, I am exclusively recruiting for roles I know will play to my strengths and where I will be successful. So let me share a few reasons why I am confident that I will thrive in this role at your company.

> (Point 1) "First, I know that I thrive when thinking both creatively and analytically—I enjoy diving into the data, solving

complicated problems in a fast-paced and project-based environment. I also find that I thrive when working with high-performing colleagues to deliver for clients. These are some of the primary reasons I am targeting consulting as a career move.

(Point 2) "Second, when I think about the various industries that consultants work in, I am particularly drawn to technology because of the rapid rate of change and ambiguity that I would encounter. Also, given my most recent role, I have an empathy for leaders in the tech space and understand their pain points.

(Point 3) "Lastly, while tech consulting is my career target, your firm is my top choice for several reasons. I'll start with the people. In visiting with people like Monisha and Tarun from the New York office, I'm absolutely wowed by the caliber of colleagues I would be working alongside and learning from in your firm. Also, it's the projects and clients. From an information session I attended last month, I got a peek behind the curtain of some of the work you all are doing in the Chicago and New York offices. I'd be thrilled to land in either. Bringing it all together, it's about mission and culture. Your commitment to being a firm known for excellent work and as leaders in socially responsible business practices speaks to the core of why I came to business school in the first place. I believe companies have an opportunity to drive value that is more than just bottom-line profit.

(Conclusion) "So, for these reasons and many more, I am so grateful to be here today, visiting with you about this opportunity. Truly, it would be a thrill to join your firm, and I'd be eager to work with you all."

This example above works for a variety of reasons, but let's focus on the structure and tone. First, the structure is logical for both the speaker and listener. Rather than defend that you deserve to be considered for a position, in this example, you are earnestly revealing to the interviewer the logical thought process and intentionality behind your career search. The idea being that you (the interviewee) are making a rational and convincing explanation for why the interviewer should believe you are a good fit for this position, this company, and this industry.

Second, the tone is right because it allows the interviewee—you—to make confident claims with a sense of humility and vulnerability. This assures the interviewer that you have done your due diligence and know your "why." It also conveys that you are approaching the position from a posture of good-natured enthusiasm.

After an interviewer has made sense of who you are (e.g., "walk me through your résumé") and why you are interviewing (i.e., "why did you apply?"), the person will naturally begin inquiring about your prior experience and probable success in the role the organization is seeking to fill. While some interviews will include a series of case questions to measure things like quantitative reasoning, for our purposes, we will focus on behavioral interview questions.

Below, are a few of my must-prepare behavioral interview questions, especially for anyone pursuing a corporate role. I could make the list a mile long, but then so could you by simply searching the web. I focus on these questions first because I believe they allow you to start developing stories that you can adapt for the myriad questions that an interviewer may ask you:

- **Leading others:**
  - Tell me about a time you led a team through a difficult challenge.

- Tell me about a time you demonstrated leadership without positional authority.

Solving problems:

- Tell me about a time you solved a complicated problem using data and thinking creatively.

- Tell me about a time that your intuition was not aligned with the data.

Managing conflict:

- Tell me about a time you worked in a team and had to manage a conflict.

- Tell me about a time you had a difficult conversation or disagreement with a client, colleague, or manager.

Influencing others:

- Tell me about a time you changed the mind of a decision maker or group of people.

- Tell me about a time that you advocated for an unpopular opinion.

Overcoming challenges:

- Tell me about a time that you faced a challenge or weakness you had to push yourself hard to overcome.

- Tell me about a time that you failed forward, meaning you made a mistake but managed to recover from it or learned a vital lesson.

As you read this list of possible interview prompts, I hope you started imagining several stories you might tell.

The next step is determining how to tell your story in a way that would make sense to someone who may not know you well, much less have any real working knowledge of your life and work experiences. For these reasons, a lot of people will try to utilize promising frameworks for responding to interview questions.

One popular method encourages individuals to answer questions by speaking to the Situation, Task, Action, and Result. It's an effective structure because it is commonly known and easy to follow. Some companies will even encourage candidates to utilize this or a similar method because it helps with timing and predictability for both the interviewer and interviewee. Conceptually, the method makes good sense. Operationally, however, the structure often leaves the interviewee struggling to open and close responses effectively, causing the interview to lack a conversational tone. Without a solid opening and closing, a story following this format feels like a song with no intro and outro to set the mood and to leave you feeling good at the end.

I find that most people do a good job identifying a smart story, but they do not prepare the content and delivery very well, causing them to sound unattached from the moment and a bit robotic. I often tell clients, "You have good material, and now we need to tell it better. I want you to get off the courtroom witness stand and into the coffee shop with a friend." To help people do that, I developed a modified approach for my clients to use. My method doesn't have a fancy acronym, but it works, and so I encourage you to use it:

- **Introduction/alignment:** Connect with the theme of the question. Align with the spirit of the prompt, perhaps revealing a worldview or perspective to set a tone for how you approach related situations generally.

- **Context/situation:** Introduce a single event that will serve as representative, providing only the context necessary to dive into the story.

- **Problem/task:** Emphasize the crux of the problem you (and your team) were facing. As this is likely the middle of your story, be sure you are keeping your listener engaged by giving this part of the story some spark. You can do this by pulling your listener in as you emphasize the drama in your story. For example, you might say, "As you can imagine, Trey, this was quite challenging for our team, given we didn't yet have a manager or know who was supposed to be taking the lead on this project." The listener must understand and feel the challenge you faced during this situation, or else your action and result will fall flat.

- **Approach/action/solution:** Explain the action you decisively took and give a quick reference to why this was the most logical and appropriate thing to do.

- **Results/impact:** State the benefits and/or consequences, whether that be to a client, your company, your team, the bottom line, or yourself.

- **Lessons/conclusion:** Conclude with the lessons you learned and how this experience has sharpened and readied you for the opportunities ahead.

Here's an example of this method in action. It's imperfect and lacks specificity, but it gives you the gist and draws your attention to the structure and tone. Suppose an interviewer gives you this interview prompt: "Tell me about a time that you faced a challenge/weakness you had to push yourself hard to overcome." Following my structure, your response might flow like this:

- **Introduction/alignment:** "I love this question, Trey, because everything I am today is because I kept saying yes to challenges. The challenge of moving multiple times in my life, learning multiple languages, working my way through college, and coming to the United States for work. All these challenges have made me the person I am, and the same can be true for workplace challenges."

- **Context/situation:** "I want to tell you about a particular challenge that I worked through that has made the difference in my career. About two years ago, during a performance evaluation with my manager, I reflected with her that I wanted to grow as a public speaker."

- **Problem/task:** "Now, this is noteworthy because, for most of my life, I have avoided public speaking. And truth be told, my manager had let me avoid most public speaking opportunities because she knew I didn't really like it. But I realized it was hindering my growth and potential for leadership, and I was ready to do something about it."

- **Approach/action/solution:** "So with the support of my manager, I started taking 'baby steps' by presenting critical information to key stakeholders in the organization, even giving small parts of speeches. This helped to grow my confidence to the point where I could hold my own during an entire presentation and even during the question-and-answer period after."

- **Results/impact:** "Of course, public speaking is not a skill that you develop overnight. It is something you must nurture regularly, and I continue to do so in my current role. Most recently, during an internal consulting project, I boldly volunteered to present our findings to our executive team."

- **Lessons/conclusion:** "What I hope you know about me is that whether it's learning languages or learning company cultures, or even overcoming the challenges of public speaking, I never shy away from a challenge that will develop me and help me grow. And I look forward to the kinds of obstacles and challenges that I will face in an exciting position like this one."

Ask the Right Questions

Either throughout or toward the end of the interview, the interviewer will likely give you (the interviewee) the opportunity to ask a few questions. You should always have questions to ask. To not ask questions is often a signal that you lack interest or forethought, neither of which is regarded positively by the person conducting the interview. While being prepared to ask questions is good, asking the right questions is great. Here are some quick tips on asking the interviewer questions.

First, never ask something that you could learn by searching the company website. Second, avoid questions that cause the interviewer to acknowledge your brilliance (e.g., "I'd like to understand your decline in positioning from Q2 to Q3 on vertical X, given your latest investment in R&D, which has significantly disadvantaged some of your legacy products and their positioning globally."); prove your intelligence (e.g., "Did you happen to see the latest article in the journal regarding trends in business strategy? I wonder if you find that kind of reasoning consistent with the business model here?"); or defend the company (e.g., "Why do you think me coming to work for your company is in the best interest of my career growth and potential?"). These examples are only a tad exaggerated from real ones I have heard from my clients. I think people mean well but forget interviewers are human and will not enjoy for one minute the thought of stroking your ego, proving their intelligence, or defending the company to you.

Third, unless it is standard for your industry, avoid aggressive questions like, "Now, that you've met with me, are there any concerns you have about hiring me?" And don't ask questions about the salary and benefits or next steps in the hiring process. They will tell you that information when it is available and if they want to keep talking to you. If you inadvertently irritate them by asking these questions, you may be diminishing your chances of getting the offer or being invited back for another round of interviews.

If interviewing were like dating, consider that the interviewer asked you out and wants to connect with you to see if there is good chemistry. Many interviewees misunderstand this when answering and asking questions. And this leads me to my last point: ask questions that help you finish strong, by conveying your appreciation for the interviewer and sincere desire to excel in the role. Here are some examples:

- "Trey, again thank you for making time to visit with me and allowing me a chance to ask a few questions. From what I've read and learned so far, I am really drawn to the company culture, but I'm limited in what I know, given I've never worked here. I understand you have been with the company for nearly three years. In your time here, what have you discovered to be unique and distinct about the company culture (from your previous roles)? What is something that might surprise me?"

- "If I am so fortunate to be in this role, I want to hit the ground running and drive value as quickly as possible. When you think of the highest-performing individuals you have hired, what are some common attributes and characteristics? And what advice would you offer to someone hoping to come in and excel in this role?"

Again, don't focus too much on any given word or phrase. All of that may be amended according to the specific industry, role, and company you are targeting. The main points to consider pertain to structure and tone. The questions you ask should not make you look special and hard to get. They should further connect you to the interviewer and provide assurance that you are sincere in your desire to join the team and be the ideal hire.

ESSENTIAL TAKEAWAYS

- Don't spend your valuable job-hunting time making cold contacts to people you don't know on LinkedIn (or anywhere else); instead, ask people already in your network about any possible ideas or opportunities they know about and are willing to share with you.

- Be straightforward about the fact you are exploring new opportunities and turning to them for *advice*, not help. Most people are flattered and therefore willing to give advice, whereas *helping* someone else requires more time and energy.

- Build your network by staying in touch with as many people you meet as possible—and not only when you're job hunting. Even quick communication builds much more goodwill than contacting someone you haven't talked to in years.

- Write cover letters with your specific audience in mind. Connect with your reader and explain why you're right for *this specific opportunity*.

CHAPTER 13

Communicate on the Job and Up the Ladder

The previous chapter was about communicating your way into a job. Imagine that you are now there and consider for a moment the plethora of communication opportunities you will face in your new role. With every message sent, meeting attended, or other human interaction, you are either securing or sabotaging your own career potential. This chapter and the next describe how communication essentials can help you communicate on the job and up the ladder as you pursue future opportunities and promotions. This chapter focuses on in-person communication, exploring ways to make (and continue making) good impressions, manage your messages in meetings, and maximize your executive presence. The next chapter focuses on how you can improve written messages to help you climb the ladder to further success.

MAKE GOOD FIRST IMPRESSIONS

We are socialized to believe that it is important to make a good first impression. You've likely heard and possibly said the phrase, "dress for success." Also, I remember as a kid hearing about women not leaving the house without "putting their face on." This may have just been an idiom and cultural norm during the time and place where I grew up, yet it speaks to the notion of public image and impression management.

That said, managing an image is more than just physical elements like attire and makeup. In fact, your first impression tends to set the tone for future interactions because how a person perceives you the first time you meet is how that person begins to define and make sense of you. If you join a new team and present yourself as a person who is competent, capable, and kind, your teammates will likely anticipate and expect such behavior from you in future interactions. You may find that they begin reciprocating kindness and warmth in their ongoing interactions with you because of the first impression you made on them.

On the contrary, if you present yourself as a person who is competent and capable, but standoffish, your teammates will likely anticipate and expect standoffish behavior from you in future interactions. As a result, they may be prone to reciprocating the standoffishness that they perceived from you the first time you met. In other words, the best way to begin influencing how people will define you and interact with you is to be very intentional with the first impression you make on them.

Imagine you have just been hired for an exciting new job at a company where you don't yet really know anyone. It's now your first day of work where they've even planned a lunch for everyone to meet you, but you wake up battling a severe headache and sinus pressure. Do you call in sick and risk being seen as a flake, a bad hire? Do you show up and struggle through the day and risk being seen as someone less impressive than when you were interviewed? You can imagine the thoughts and comments others might have (e.g., "Who calls in sick on day one?" or "Why is she here if she is sick? Is she trying to get all of us sick?"), which only further reminds you that it's a seemingly no-win situation.

Interestingly, much of this concern would go away if you woke up feeling sick during your second week on the job, after you had already met everyone. You might think: *It's OK, they know and like me. If I show up with a headache and just explain, they'll get it. Or, if I need to take a sick day, they'll likely understand that too. They know me by now and hopefully trust that I'd be there if I could.*

One explanation for why you should care so much about the first impressions you make is because people don't like to be wrong. Most people believe they are able to effectively observe and interpret the world around them. If they believe the car that zipped by was green, good luck convincing them it was red. If they believe the person they interviewed lacked confidence and seemed a bit odd, good luck convincing them that the person is a real winner and client-ready. People like to be right and find it easier to reinforce their beliefs than to question them. Additionally, interpreting human behavior is a bit subjective. Whereas someone can show you evidence that the car was red—proving you were wrong—in the case of observing and interpreting humans, most of the time you can keep believing whatever you want, even if you are wrong. So, the goal with first impressions is to be sure to present yourself exactly as you'd like to be seen and known, because once an impression is made it's very difficult to change it.

To be clear, creating a fake or deceptive image is wrong. But our desire to make good impressions, just like our desire to understand others' behavior, is not a bad or negative thing. These are undeniably human traits, and are as normal as checking the temperature and attempting to set the thermostat.

Moreover, you don't only make a first impression when you first accept a job; every time your job changes or you get promoted, you will likely be evaluated anew. For example, think of times you've heard someone say something like, "Well, she aced the interviews and got the job, but I guess now we'll see what she's really made of." Or "He's definitely pulled his weight as an individual contributor. It'll be interesting to see if he can hack it as a manager." For these reasons, one of the first things I tell clients when they start a new job or assume a new responsibility is, "Don't pop the champagne yet, because now the real interview begins!"

Here's an example. One of my clients, the director of digital strategy at a major technology company, recently moved laterally in her company. She was recruited by a senior leader to help lead digital strategy and planning. Even though she was highly recruited, the weeks-long interview process for her new position was grueling. Once she got the job, I reminded her that even though she had been with the company for years and was highly recruited into this role, it was still up to her to win over her new team. This is because even when people know and like you, when you jump into something new, they now have a new reason to size you up and evaluate you from a new perspective.

She told me that during the first week, she was able to shrug off some hard questions by kindly pointing out that she was new to the role and still learning the ropes. By week two of onboarding, she alerted me that she was having the "drinking from a firehose" experience, which seemed normal for a new job and especially one the size and scope of her new role. I became concerned, however, when she told me she had started repeating some phrases with her colleagues that went like, "OK, not understanding this. Remember, I'm the dumb one here." Such self-deprecating humor does have the potential benefit of a quick laugh with your new colleagues, but I knew her long-term vision for her career, and priming people to see her as "the dumb one" was not on message for her brand.

So we devised a plan that would help her stay lighthearted while confused but showcase a different side of her. When people assumed she had a working knowledge that she didn't or got too deep into the weeds on something she was unfamiliar with, she would try saying things like this:

> "Trey, if we can pause briefly, this seems like a really important concept. And I want to make sure that I understand it well enough that I could explain it to the next person we hire. So, I'd like to back up for one minute to ask some high-level questions first. For instance, when do we use this and why? . . . OK, great, just another quick question. What are some must dos and don'ts for mastering this process? Awesome. Thank you so much. I've jotted this down. And I appreciate you giving me that extra minute. As I'm learning more about what we do, I'm trying to be thoughtful about how I can help us onboard future teammates."

In this small change of how she communicated her need for more information during her onboarding period, my client was able to accomplish the critical goal of learning what she needed to know. Even more, rather than playing "the dumb one," she was able to project her willingness and alleged readiness to effectively onboard and manage future employees.

This change in how she asked for information was an easy fix that I was confident would go over well within her immediate group, but I admit I didn't foresee just how impactful it would be. Her colleagues and manager were so impressed by the approach she was taking with her onboarding that the senior leadership team eventually commissioned her to develop a digital onboarding experience for the entire division, intended to be a model that could be replicated across the entire company. One small change in messaging, and my client is now overseeing an initiative that will reach the C suite and potentially impact more than 75,000 employees.

Impression management is ongoing. Even if you have settled into your role, it is important to pull back on occasion and assess what impression you are making and reinforcing. Another one of my clients, Amanda, reflected with me that she felt less confident at work. I asked her for some indicators that told her so. We soon realized that, following a company reorganization, she was now responsible for an additional team that oversaw an area of the business she was less familiar with. She found she was using a lot of tentative language (e.g., "we may perhaps consider" and "this might be suggesting that") and unnecessarily apologizing (e.g., "sorry to bother, this will just be a minute" and "apologies for flooding your inbox") when talking with this team, and that it was starting to carry over into all of her workplace interactions. While tentative language and apologizing have their places, she had begun doing both habitually and unnecessarily.

Even though we were able to talk through it, I could tell she was still feeling a bit hopeless, as though she couldn't turn around the image she had formed. That is, until I reminded her of the power of the recency effect.[1] While the *primacy effect* suggests that individuals will emphasize a first impression when forming a perception of a person, the *recency effect* suggests that individuals will emphasize the most recent impression when forming a perception of someone. (You may be more familiar with this concept as "what have you done for me lately?")

In regard to workplace relationships, first impressions (primacy effect) are critical, and so is the last impression (recency effect) you made. Even with colleagues you've known for ages, your first impressions and your most recent impressions are more important than those that come in between.[2] Thus, my client needed to remember that the past is the past, and those impressions can't be remade. Yet she could make deliberate choices to ensure the most recent impression she made would be a great one. From there, we needed some tools in place to help her feel less tentative and more sure of herself when communicating. To do that, we established core messaging aligned with her current position and career path and then developed communication frameworks and patterns for her to follow that would ensure her future impressions would be the ones that would stick with others. If you find yourself in a situation like my client, take hope in knowing that the essentials provided in this book are here to help you make great impressions going forward.

(RE)MAKE A FIRST IMPRESSION

A couple of years ago, I got a call from a friend who is a senior leader at a telecommunications company. Her budget was gone, but major changes were hitting her organization. She wanted to know if I would do her a favor and facilitate a morale-boosting workshop for her core team. It was going to be a three-hour workshop just before Thanksgiving. Under normal circumstances, I would have charged top dollar to develop and deliver a three-hour workshop for a major telecommunications company, especially around the holidays. But the date that she needed worked with my schedule, and I was happy to help a friend. So I agreed.

On the day of the workshop, I was rushed and arrived with only 30 minutes to spare. I met my friend outside the conference site. The participants were inside eating lunch before our session. She walked me in to survey the room. I couldn't see a projector and screen, so I asked how the technology was going to work. She told me, "Oh, you wouldn't believe what that was going to cost, so I hope you are OK to go without tech."

As you can imagine, giving a pro bono talk for three hours without the benefit of using the slides I had prepared for the event was less than desirable. But that was OK. I don't mind a challenge. I walked outside and developed a new game plan quickly. I came back in, poured a coffee (fortunately, their budget could afford all the coffee that I was going to need!), and sat down with the group as they wrapped up their lunch. My friend whispered that she would do an introduction, and that would be my cue to get started.

Her speech to introduce me to the audience went something like this:

> "Hey, hope you liked lunch. Denise picked it, so if you didn't like it, blame her, not me. [No one laughed.] On a serious note, though, we're having major changes at work. We all feel them, and it's not all that fun. So I wanted today to be a time where we could come together, discuss the changes, and develop some new protocols for how to manage them. This afternoon is now a time to bond as a team. I tried to get us one of those fancy, expensive speakers . . . but we all know that we have no budget. So, this is what we got—Trey. [She pointed to me. And, again no one laughed.] Trey, the floor is yours."

Honest to goodness, while I may have missed the precise language, that was the gist of her introduction of me. I don't think she meant any harm. I truly believe she was trying to be funny, but it flopped, and it left people in the room confused. I could see their faces as I sat down among them. They didn't know what to think. Unless they had magically guessed that she was being humorous, they likely assumed the next three hours with me were going to be awful and that not even the person in charge of the event wanted me there.

The seating was a U-shape. I made my way to the top of the U, and I said how glad I was to be there with them all, especially as they made sense of some turbulent times. I then made a joke saying, "What my friend doesn't know is that her boss promised me and my family a lifetime of free internet, cable, and phone service, which is far better than a one-time speaker's fee." The crowd ate it up. I then talked a little bit about how I enjoy working with companies during change management and that, while there are similar experiences, no two stories are the same. Within two minutes, I had undone the horrible introduction and bad setup that I had been given.

Experiences like this one urge me to remind you of two things. First, when given the opportunity, always set people up for success. Help others make a great first impression. Ask if they have something prepared that they want you to use when introducing them. If not, ask them for some general direction about how they want to be introduced. Your job is to alley-oop someone to slam-dunk the ball. If you do your introduction well, the audience will be confident in the credibility of the new person; then it is up to that individual to maintain, possibly elevate, the credibility you provided them.

Second, when being introduced, be thoughtful about the biography or introductory remarks you want given on your behalf, and don't be afraid to ask, perhaps even insist, that it be used. Your introduction should not overpromise what you will deliver but should highlight why you are the ideal candidate to deliver what you are there to do.

But more than just preparing a quality biography and introductory remarks, there are important takeaways from the experience I had when giving the workshop for my friend's company. There are always unexpected curveballs at work, which require you to be nimble and adaptable. You will have many instances that require you to pivot and change course, and usually you must do so without showing your frustration. People will use humor at your expense, even if they don't have any ill intent, and it will often be in your best interest to stay composed, laugh it off, and keep focus on the real issues at hand. You will have to think and respond quickly to undo someone else's poor messaging, usually while simultaneously protecting the feelings of the person who miscommunicated. As a communicator, scenarios like these require you to be nimble and adapt easily, which is easier to do when you have ready-made messaging frameworks at your disposal (provided later in the chapter and throughout the book).

LIKE ME, LIKE YOU

There is an old adage, "it's not what you know, it's who you know." Renowned communication scholar John Daly used to tell us in class, "Actually, it's not who knows you. It's who likes you." He is right. There are plenty of people you may know but not necessarily trust to water your plants, much less offer them a job. This is an important lesson in navigating a career, and one that I help my clients with regularly.

As an example, one of my clients had recently been recruited out of his business strategy role with a global consumer goods company to take a new business strategy opportunity with one of the big five multinational technology companies. In fact, he was being hired by a major technology company to spearhead its relationship with another major technology company. It's a high-pressure job, with about a billion dollars a year on the line. He was very enthusiastic about the role, and we knew that his success in the position would depend on multiple individuals—both at his company and the partner company—trusting him and liking him. So some of our early goals in working together were to establish strong ties with people in his immediate orbit, especially his key stakeholders.

Unfortunately, his approach started to slip, and in his first weeks on the job, he was reporting back to me that people he worked closest with were a little standoffish. Upon further discussion, the problem was obvious to me. My client was showing up to meetings with the desire to prove his competence and readiness (which is not altogether bad). He was burning the midnight oil in order to arrive each day having solved all the foreseeable riddles. The problem was that he was so insistent on winning others over by demonstrating how smart and capable he was that he was alienating himself (like a classroom know-it-all) and missing opportunities to make any real connection with his new colleagues. I don't blame him. He wanted to impress everyone, hoping it would somehow make them like him and see his value.

But that is not how *liking* works. In reality (and especially because he was new to the team), he needed to pull back on being the problem solver and emphasize that he was an active listener, willing to make time to learn what he needed to learn and establish meaningful connections with the team.

I asked him what it would take to know he was liked, and he said normal things like, "Well, if they smiled when they saw me or asked about my day." I asked him when he last smiled at any of them or asked about their days. Silence. I told him the truth: "You've got to give what you want to get. You've been showing up to meetings to prove how smart you are to a bunch of people you were hired to support

and champion. Then you are disappointed when they don't smile, say thanks, and ask about your day?!" We had major work to do, and I'm glad we did it because everything is now running smoothly for my client.

The biggest takeaway that I can share with you is this—liking begets liking. If you want others to like you, you must first communicate how much you like them. This doesn't mean you walk up telling people, "I like you!" It may simply mean a warm smile and kind word at the start of a meeting, affirming other people's ideas, or sending a quick note of appreciation from time to time.

Think of how easy it has become in the information age to be a self-absorbed and distracted human. On average, people don't have time to figure out if they like you, but they are highly adept at perceiving if others like and respect them. So make it easy for those around you, and choose to like them first. Give them your polite smile when they enter or exit a meeting, and nod respectfully and affirmingly when they speak ideas that you agree with. When others perceive that you like and respect them, they will be more likely to reciprocate in kind. At worst, you have given a smile and kind word to someone who didn't reciprocate. Is that so bad? What is the better alternative? In most cases, liking begets liking. In other words, the people you demonstrate liking toward *should* follow your lead and like you in return. And even when they don't, you've learned invaluable information about that person.

MANAGE YOUR BRAND

BMW asserts that its cars are the "Ultimate Driving Machine." Meanwhile, we are to believe "there is no substitute" for a Porsche. Institutions of higher education are quite proud, too. "What starts here changes the world," claims The University of Texas at Austin. And really, do I even need to tell you the Nike slogan? Companies aren't alone in the claim for fancy taglines and smart branding. What's yours? Don't have one? The time to get one is now.

The sooner you know your tagline and brand yourself, the sooner you can begin following your own North Star up the ladder of your career. Mine is perfect for me:

> Trey Guinn is a lifelong learner and full-time educator. As a lifelong learner, I wake each day with keen awareness that I ought to choose a posture of humility and gratitude, maintain sincere curiosity, and demonstrate my desire to listen to and learn from others. Concurrently, as a full-time

educator, I embrace the grand responsibility and life calling as a person in a position to teach, coach, and model
the way for others.

One might wonder why any of this branding and cute slogan stuff
matters. Here is why. Just like organizations, we as individuals are regularly called to do several things all in several directions amid several distractions. With so much to manage, it's easy to betray a critical
asset—the entity. Without a branding convention, a clear declaration of who we are and why we exist, it is easy to get lost in the sea of
stuff and mismanage the brand. If BMW enters the arena of economy
vehicles, it can toss its "Ultimate Driving Machine" claim. And if UT-
Austin's deans start printing diplomas for any dollar thrown their way,
they can abandon that whole "changing the world" mantra. Instead,
those slogans and branding instill a shared purpose for all who work
at such organizations, a trump card in the middle of meetings when
people offer bogus ideas that are inconsistent and off-brand. For me,
the personal claim to be a lifelong learner and full-time educator keeps
me humble, grateful, eager. So what about you?

To begin the process of knowing and owning your brand, consider
a few things. A personal brand is very similar to a corporate brand. It
should reflect the values you embrace and how you express those values. Like a company brand communicates distinguishing value to cus-
tomers, a personal brand ought to communicate unique identity and
value. It is like the hook to a great story.

To develop your personal brand, you must first become introspective, reflecting on your strengths and motivations. While much of
the advice I give professionals is to keep doors open, there is a reality
to knowing yourself, your goals, and how you thrive. No one person

can do everything and own all the things at work. You must get honest about who you are, even as you evolve, and allow that to influence your forecasting of where you see yourself in the near future.

For example, a client of mine, a vice president at a startup in the San Francisco Bay Area, was up for promotion. His organization was about to go public; simultaneously he was being asked to manage the acquisition of a smaller boutique operation. He had previously felt very sure of himself when showing up to work, but now he was beginning to feel unsure of how to manage the varying dynamics. He was still leading people and projects but now had to be mindful of the stressors that come with going public. And he also needed to figure out how to onboard people (including the CEO) from the acquired company. Being led, leading others, and trying to smoothly transition in an existing team (most of whom were feeling less than inspired about the changes) are challenging dynamics to manage on a daily basis—especially when you are jockeying for a promotion and dependent on positive feedback from the varying parties.

During one of our sessions together, I played a Range Rover commercial for him. At first, he looked confused. But as the commercial was running, I explained that he was that Range Rover in the commercial. The essence and core of the vehicle never changes, even while crossing a river, traversing a mountain, speeding down a highway, or being valeted at a fancy gala.

Part of showing up at work when wearing many hats and operating cross-functionally is learning how to own the core of who you are while also emphasizing your different strengths for the right occasion. If being customer-obsessed and self-assured is core to your personal brand, you can exercise that as a decisive, no-nonsense leader in one meeting and an active-listener, curious leader in the next.

Internalizing this concept—that the engine and essence of the vehicle never changes, but how you drive and the features you emphasize must adapt for the occasion—helped my client navigate some challenging predicaments, mostly with winning over the incoming CEO.

Another example of training someone to think of his presence like an all-purpose vehicle came when I was working with a relatively new university president. A successful academic and recipient of large research grants, he was now the figurehead presiding over a highly ranked university. He already had a speechwriter and staff to help him prepare for large events and smaller gatherings. I was called in to help with his speech anxiety and general quirkiness as a communicator.

Before our meeting, I had watched footage of him presenting to various crowds, and it was clear to me that he had no problem playing the part of an academic and sounding intelligent. He had no problem with winning over fellow academics and elites, but this was not the right tone or presence for audiences needing to see a curious or compassionate leader. He clearly struggled with shifting gears and sounding like anything other than a stuffy smart guy in the room.

Our first meeting was rough, and I felt we got nowhere. The problem was that he was too protected. His staff was nervous I would critique their writing or somehow offend him, and so they stayed in the room with us. They continued to invade our time together, preventing any chance for an honest and raw conversation.

For the second meeting, I boldly requested his staff give us privacy together. My client and his team acted unsure of this, and so I knew I needed to act quickly before he called his staff back in or dismissed me altogether. My client's problem was that he communicated in only one style, and this was hindering his ability to connect with audiences. I needed him to embrace that his role required him to stretch and adapt his communication style, and I needed him to believe that he was capable of doing so. But I couldn't simply tell him that. He had to see it for himself.

To do this, I asked him about the last time he played with or read to kids. He was totally confused by my question, almost aghast that I would waste his time in such a way, but eventually he mentioned to me that he had read a holiday-themed book to his grandchildren during a recent family gathering. I asked him to tell me about the story. I then asked him to tell me about the story while imagining that he was reading to a sea of children in an old-fashioned toy store. Over the course of the questions, although he was puzzled by my asking, I saw his eyes twinkle and a smile beginning to form. To my delight and his surprise, this was working.

So then I went for it. I called him over to the podium, handed him the draft of his speech for the following week, and told him to read the speech to a room of children. I reminded him, "This reading is not to diminish your presidential status; it is to showcase that twinkle in the eye and loving smile that comes out when you imagine your grandson is in the audience."

He decided not to kick me out of his office. Over the next few months working together, we stretched his executive presence to be more versatile. He learned to adapt appropriately for the occasion and audience, while never betraying his core brand as an intelligent and capable leader.

My hope for you is that you will not try to fit your current or future roles into your existing communication style. Instead, see your communication style like a muscle that can grow to meet the weight of the communication opportunities that arise in your current or future roles. Simple exercises like reading aloud while picturing different audiences (e.g., school-aged children, congressional leaders, an all-hands business meeting) will allow you to discover and strengthen your speaking voice, so that next time you speak up in a meeting you have even more confidence in your ability to maximize your presence and not betray your brand.

MAKE MEETINGS MATTER AND MAXIMIZE EXECUTIVE PRESENCE

I work with some smart clients, and across the board, one of the challenges that many of them face is knowing how to show up in meetings. Of course, they know how to arrive, but I mean *show up* in the presentational sense of the phrase. Many of my clients feel flat-footed when asked to give a status update on a project. Or they feel a little caught off-guard when called on to provide input on a given topic. In most cases, it's not because they lack awareness or ability to contribute. Instead, for most, it's because they struggle to streamline their thoughts and share them in a meaningful way. Additionally, they may feel intimidated by individuals in the meeting. When asked for an update on a particular project, they find themselves saying things like:

> "Ugh. Well, there is not much to report on, except that the team has been doing many things to try and understand what needs to be our focus coming up as we continue to consider where we are at versus where we need to be in time for . . ."

I think most will agree that this message is vague and lacking any real substance, which of course is no benefit to the audience. Equally problematic is that communicating like this is a missed opportunity for the communicator to establish credibility and flex his or her executive presence. So years ago, following the wisdom of communication essentials, I developed some conceptual frameworks to help people *show up* to meetings better prepared. Obviously, I don't know the specifics of what you talk about during your meetings, but I can still teach you smart ways for *how* to talk about what you talk about. I've already described *what, so what, now what* (and *recap, request, remind* is in the next chapter). Here's another one that my clients find really helpful: the *what, why, how* technique. Imagine if in the example above, the person who was asked for a status update simply responded in this format:

> "Right now, we are laser-focused on resolving X [the what] because all data and indicators tell us that is our most critical pain point [the why], and our smartest approach so far is to X, Y, and Z." [the how]

I'm going to show the utility of the *what, why, how* technique across a few domains. Let's start with an easy, personal example. Imagine that on the way home, you call your partner and say:

> "We should eat pizza tonight for dinner [the what] because it's been over a month, and the kids would love it. [the why] I can pick it up on my way home from our favorite place. I've even got a discount!" [the how]

Now, imagine you are in a meeting, and your manager asks for a performance update or explanation of numbers. You may know your numbers backward and forward but still struggle with how to package and present the information to a room of people. However, having a simple framework to speak from might make all the difference. Here's your framework: tell them what matters, why it matters, and how you plan/recommend addressing it:

> "I am happy to provide an update for everyone. As we look at the data, we see that not all regions are performing the same. [the what]

"With a closer look, there are some obvious explanations. For instance, restaurants in X region have yet to reopen. This factor is important to consider, as it helps to explain—at least in part—why we aren't seeing the numbers we forecasted the year prior. [the why]

"Given this, and our inability to predict when restaurants in the region will reopen, I recommend that we adjust our forecast by X." [the how]

While this framework may not account for the complexity of your next communication dilemma, it will allow you to stay focused on the core of your message in only a few words, which is your best bet for maintaining executive presence in a fast-paced meeting.

For example, imagine you are in a meeting and the group is leaning toward adjusting the deliverable date to the client. If you have only a few seconds to recommend something different, you might choose to say something like this:

"We need to stick to the original timeline for this deliverable [the what] because we promised the client and our reputation is on the line. [the why] I am confident that we can do this if we get one more head count from X and if we remain diligent in our communication with the design team." [the how]

In this case, your objective may not be to hit a home run with one comment. Likely though, with a clear, concise, and compelling message, you can showcase your competent and confident self, effectively reopening the debate.

It is worth noting that quantitative evidence and specificity will be your friend in most cases. Likewise, when possible, I encourage people to provide a proposed impact following the *how*. So just like in most of my examples, focus on the style and structure more than the specific words. There are plenty of benefits to using the *what, why, how* structure when communicating. Namely, whereas many individuals may be prone to talking about their ideas aloud (externally processing information) and providing circular reasoning, the purpose of this framework is to help you streamline your ideas into clear, concise messages that help audiences process information logically. It's another simple and smart way to make meetings matter and maximize your executive presence.

STAY ON MESSAGE; AVOID PITFALLS

All smart politicians, public figures, crisis communicators, or media personalities know to never take a stage or get near a camera without having prepared their talking points and considering potential communication pitfalls. Depending on the situation, someone may have one message to convey or many.

For example, consider athletes who always say the worst things on camera versus athletes who always seem to pivot away from negative talk and back to simple and smart messages. There are five basic things that athletes can almost always talk about and pivot to when unsure about a question thrown their way. Those five are: worthy opponents, great coaching, outstanding teammates, personal responsibility, and gratitude for the fans. At the end of a game, suppose a sideline reporter asks an athlete to comment on what happened during the play in the third quarter. Here's a great response:

> "I need to see the footage, but I want to tell you that we played a great team today, and we have a lot of respect for their

organization. Our coaches knew what it would take to win this game, they prepared us well, and I'm so proud of our team for showing up here and playing like we did. I'll be up and at it early in the morning, watching the footage, and doing the work necessary to play my very best next week because that's what we do and that's what these awesome fans deserve! Thank you, have a great night!"

This is how athletes avoid pitfalls and stay on message. Politicians on cable news do the same thing.

Strategic communicators of all kinds understand the importance of staying on message. Because you also have a brand to protect—your own—it's important that you do the same. Perhaps you do this at times and don't even realize it. Friends, colleagues, and couples will sometimes coach one another on what to say or not to say. Imagine a scenario where a couple is driving to a dinner party, and you remind each other about what to mention and not mention (e.g., "don't talk about colleges because Ravi is still upset that he didn't get into X University"; "don't talk about money because Jie just lost his job"; "be sure to mention how good the desserts are because Margot baked all the pies").

Before a meeting or event, I encourage my clients to operate like the athlete just mentioned. Specifically, I recommend doing three things:

1. First, draft five smart talking points (e.g., great coaches, personal responsibility) per any given situation (e.g., postgame interview).

2. Second, think of at least five communication pitfalls (e.g., being asked about a peculiar call by a referee) to avoid during any given situation.

3. Lastly, connect the dots from potential pitfall topics to your preferred talking points.

For a visual, consider your fingertips. Imagine having your top five talking points on your left hand and your top five pitfalls on your right hand. Now, imagine taking those talking points on your left hand and using them to maneuver out of the pitfalls on your right. For instance, if you're asked a pitfall question like: "What do you think of the referee calling foul with one second left?" You should respond like this: "I trust that everyone is doing their job to the best of their ability. I didn't have the view that others had, so I'll let our coaching staff answer that one. For me, I'm focused on playing the best I can for our team and our fans." Ignoring pitfalls with an answer like "I don't know" is better than saying something awful. But even better than dodging the question is when you can convert potential pitfalls into your desired talking points.

To come up with your core talking points, consider parts of your current and future role. Consider organizational principles and industry ideals or trends that you wish to be known for championing—for example:

- Do you wish to be recognized as a customer-obsessed leader?

- Do you want to be known as someone willing to take a deep dive into the data?

- Do you want to be recognized as the ideal candidate for the role and responsibilities you wish to have? If so, how would you talk and what questions would you ask in boardroom meetings?

- Do you want to be seen as a thoughtful leader in your industry? If so, what topics would you bring up or ask about at a cocktail party?

As you process through questions like these, write down at least five talking points. For example, a dutiful scholar who hopes to develop a reputation as someone equally committed to student learning might make this a talking point:

> "If we are serious about student learning and promoting better scholarship, we should think more inclusively and develop a funding model that accounts for faculty-student mentorship, which we know can yield better research and is effective for training future scholars, both of which are principles this institution was built on."

Imagine a marketing leader who is meeting with the executive leadership team. The person is known and respected for having a pulse on the customer, but she realizes her intuition alone won't be enough to persuade leadership to promote her to the next level. She knows the company is looking for someone with strong quantitative skills who makes data-informed decisions. In this case, she might make this one of her talking points:

> "Anecdotal evidence and intuition benefited us greatly this past quarter. We ought to take these insights and let them define and refine an analytical approach to optimize our marketing spends and help us make data-informed decisions."

Similar talking points can be used when avoiding pitfalls or being pigeonholed as someone who relies on intuition. Imagine she is in a meeting with senior leaders, and one says to her, "You seem to have good intuition for what our target market is thinking, what do you advise?" She may take this as a compliment. Or, because she is trying to boost her credibility as a marketing leader with quantitative skills who makes data-informed decisions, she might see the compliment as problematic to the identity she is seeking to elevate. In this case, to avoid the pitfall and emphasize her talking point, she could say something like:

> "Thank you. I appreciate that you recognize my commitment to our customer, which is why I can't advise going with our gut on this one. It would behoove us to take a deeper dive and gather some additional insights before making the final call."

There is no trickery or magic with developing your talking points and preventing pitfalls. It becomes relatively easy the more frequently you analyze your audience and focus on knowing your brand and goals as a communicator. The problem is that many individuals figure out what they should have said after the camera is off or after they leave the meeting. You've likely heard the phrase "an ounce of prevention is worth a pound of cure." The same can be said for communication. Rather than spending hours playing cleanup after saying the wrong thing, you are better off taking a few minutes to prep your talking points, predict possible pitfalls, and figure out how to make each interaction work to your advantage.

ESSENTIAL TAKEAWAYS

- First interactions with someone will set the tone for future interactions.

- Impression management is ongoing: even if you have settled into your role, it is important to pull back on occasion and assess what impression you are making and reinforcing.

- More important than being known is being liked by influential people. If you want others to like you, you must first communicate how much you like them.

- A personal brand should reflect the values you embrace and how you express those values.

- When asked to report on something in meetings, use this simple framework: describe *what* happened, *why* it's important, and *how* you should move forward.

- To help you stay on message, be prepared by identifying five smart talking points and five potential pitfalls and then connect the dots from potential pitfall topics to your preferred talking points, so you can answer tough questions with what *you* want to say.

Improve Your Digital Communication

Now that you are in your job and making some strong first in-person impressions, it's time to make sure that you are helping, not hindering, yourself digitally. Your personal brand has the potential to elevate or evaporate each time you click send. With the rapid shift to hybrid work and endless communication platforms at our disposal comes

Your personal brand has the potential to

Elevate   or   Evaporate

the blessing and burden of a more complicated digital communication environment. This chapter focuses on how to make good impressions digitally and encourages you to think twice before firing off your next message.

MAKE GOOD IMPRESSIONS DIGITALLY

Before the ubiquity of online communication, a great teammate may have been described as good at his or her job, easy to get along with, and willing to cover your shift if an emergency were to pop up. And while we know that much of making a good first impression in the workplace happens by having the right vibe when interacting in person and virtually, another critical factor is being a consummate teammate in digital communication.

Regardless of format, your impact as a communicator is rarely neutral. You are either making a positive or negative impression. The goal should be to maximize positive impressions and minimize negative impressions. Doing so does not require you to always say yes, people please, or give in to every request. In fact, you can easily avoid some negative impression traps by remembering a few simple practices described next.

Don't Leave People Hanging

Unless someone has made an out-of-office announcement, it is safe to assume that a message will be seen within 24 hours. So, if you receive a message requesting support but know you can't get to it for another 72 hours, it might be perfectly fine to wait 72 hours before completing the task. But that doesn't mean you should wait that entire time before acknowledging the request. It usually only takes 30 seconds to reply and let people know you need that time. To deny them a heads-up is to leave people hanging and wondering if you ever received the message.

Give People What They Need to Succeed

If you know the precise source, link, or file your recipient will need to reference, it's better to share the right one than assume people will find it with guided instructions. If you have a file with formatting that may look different across devices, take the extra step to send it as a PDF. Conversely, if you know that people will want to easily manipulate the information in the file, send the original, editable version. If you want people to avoid misunderstandings and remember specific decisions made during a meeting, take the additional step of sending a recap message. If you want to avoid confusion about meeting details, share a meeting invite that includes all the necessary information (e.g., what is it about; who should attend; when, where, and how the meeting will be held; etc.).

Practice Empathy

Digital notifications are never-ending. Virtual meetings overtake the day. No matter how important your issue may be, recognize that people are exhausted. Individuals desperately want a spare minute for a bio-break or a chance to step outside. When someone shows up two minutes late to your scheduled meeting or decides to drop in two minutes early, give that person the benefit of the doubt. It's possible your colleague just needed a glass of water and a moment to think. For this reason, one of the most important things we can do when establishing positive rapport digitally is to practice empathy. While solving a major work crisis is important, it's possible that your greatest contribution to the meeting is flashing a warm smile and sharing an encouraging word.

There are numerous things we ought to consider when striving to make strong impressions digitally. Specific tips for how to be a savvy digital communicator will evolve alongside the actual tools utilized. But the critical reminder is to be audience-centered and remember to "do unto others as you would have done unto you."

ESTABLISH NORMS FOR DIGITAL COMMUNICATION

Make life easier for you and those you collaborate with by establishing clear communication norms, and then stick to them! People have their preferences for how they send, receive, store, and access information. And when working independently, that is their prerogative. But when you are collaborating with others and joining forces as a work group or team, establishing and adhering to a communication code of the road is a must. Here are some practices that many groups I consult with tend to find standard operating procedure:

- Internal messaging (e.g., Slack) is ideal for two people or work teams who need to convey time-sensitive information or converse quickly about an urgent matter. Pro tip: While a misspelled word and a little personality can be expected in an instant messaging environment, you would be wise to avoid building a reputation as the unprofessional jokester. Also, don't data-dump or expect after-hour responses unless that expectation is established in advance.

- Emailing is ideal for important, timely information and is helpful for establishing a record of communication, especially when a response can be delayed up to 24 hours or not required at all. Pro tip: If you wouldn't feel comfortable cc'ing your local news reporter and county sheriff on your email, think twice before sending it.

- Texting is ideal for individuals and groups who have mutually agreed that they would like to be contacted for urgent messages or personal/professional banter. Pro tip: It might be your personal phone, but that doesn't mean you won't be held to professional standards.

THINK TWICE BEFORE YOU TYPE, AND THINK AGAIN BEFORE YOU SEND

Before you go to bed and when you wake up in the morning, are you more likely to call someone or check your emails and other messages? We know the answer. Now, pause for a moment and imagine how many messages you convey in one day, strictly from the keyboards across your devices. And if you are like me, go ahead and include the messages you voice-dictate to Siri. The point is that people communicate with their fingers a lot, perhaps much more than they realize.

It's easy to go into autopilot with our written communication because the sound of emails sent and received, Slack notifications, text alerts, and more have become like background engine noise and car horns of the modern workday. But there are reasons to take your written communication quite seriously. For one, the messages you send and receive will outlive you and if not handled with care could be the death of your career. Second, many of us are expected to produce written communication that is of high quantity and quality. Long ago, Amazon founder Jeff Bezos insisted his leadership team abandon slide deck presentations in favor of narrative writing. The thought was that many people can learn to give a slick presentation and win an audience without substance, but writing clarifies thought, and when people pause to read and then debate the merits of an argument better decisions will be made. At Amazon, when putting forward a proposal, a highly refined, six-page memo is standard practice.

Bezos's insistence on narrative writing at Amazon ought to clue us into a couple of things. First, the written word is asynchronous, allowing you (the writer) time to be intentional, vet your ideas, and perfect your message before you share it. Amazonians drafting a six-pager may spend hours upon hours drafting their memos. But for most of us, firing off an email or instant message may take only seconds. However, the fingerprint for each is just as damning. While a sloppy spoken word may be forgotten or batted away as "Oops, that came out wrong," a message typed and sent carries a presumed level of intentionality.

Second, because written words are perceived with more intentionality and carry your fingerprint, if you're serious about protecting and promoting your brand, you need to make sure not to dilute their impact and overexpose or sabotage yourself with sloppy and unnecessary emails or messaging. For those who feel compelled to live with their fingers at the keyboard, the following paragraphs offer some general rules of thumb (no pun intended).

Proofread Every Message

You should proofread every message you send, not only to ensure that it says what you want it to say, but to prevent embarrassing mistakes.

For example, during my first year on the job as an assistant professor, my dean called me into a meeting about the curriculum at the last minute. She texted, "Are you coming?" to be sure I had gotten the invite. I was multitasking while walking toward the meeting and dictated my response via Siri. I said, "Almost there. Just a sec." I'm not sure why I said that, as it seems very unprofessional now. Even worse, Siri didn't understand "sec" and assumed I meant "sex." I didn't know I had sent that until well after the meeting, and I was mortified. The dean knew my intent and we laughed about it later, but I learned my lesson. Proofread. Every time.

And this leads me to a related stopgap to help keep you from making similar mistakes. Fill in the "To" line last. Most people start their emails by completing the "To" line and then the "Subject" line and then proceeding to compose the email and click send. A better rule of thumb is to compose your message, refine it, provide a subject that matches the refined message, and then, at the end, add the recipient. This order places smart guardrails to potentially prevent you from sending your message until you're sure it says what you want it to say.

Don't Drink and Type

Over the past decade, I have received dozens of early morning urgent requests from clients needing some help *fixing* an email or message that they sent while intoxicated the night before. They'll say something like, "I got buzzy, was feeling confident, and overpromised a client." Other scenarios of drunk typing tend to deal with "sounded flirty but was just joking" or "probably came off aggressive but didn't mean it." The point being that the drink bone should not be connected to the work bone. If drinking and driving can wreck vehicles, drinking and working can wreck careers. I have clients who have vowed that they will text me and put their phone away before they pick up their first drink. If it works for them, it can work for you. Use the buddy system. If friends don't let friends drink and drive, they shouldn't let them drink and work!

Have a Point; Get to It Quickly

All around us, people are constantly multitasking. If everyday events and meetings are the primary activities people are doing, your emails and messages are people's secondary activities. People walk to the restroom and check messages. They eat lunch and check messages. They are in meetings and check messages. They are at their kids' recitals and check messages. In other words, your memo, message, or email is not some work of art that readers will pause for and treasure. It is that next thing they are reading while probably doing something else. So, to make their life easier, simplify your message. Make it the easiest "other thing" they've ever had to do.

In Chapter 9, I described the pyramid structure as a smart way to make your request up front and then methodically explain how you got to that point. This pyramid structure has great utility, especially when making a business case to executive leaders and decision makers. For other situations, you may wish to utilize other frameworks. I will share a couple now.

The first framework is *recap, request, and remind (or wrap up)*:

- *Recap:* start your email with a one- or two-sentence note about why you have invaded the person's inbox.

- *Request:* Following the recap or problem statement, jump to the *request* or recommendation you are making.

- *Remind:* After you have outlined the why for your request or recommendation, close with a wrap-up or *reminder* of what the person can expect next.

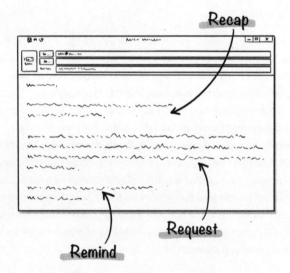

When following this flow, a message may read something like this (which is written in a longer/friendlier tone):

Hey Mike,

Regarding the open position for SVP, the committee met on Monday and still feels positive about candidates one and four. *(recap)*

Please let me know as soon as possible if Friday still works for scheduling meetings with each. *(request)*

Confirming this will help the committee plan activities for next week, which I will send to you by the end of the day tomorrow. *(remind)*

Sincerely, Trey

Sometimes, though, you don't have a clear ask or request, yet you still must provide an important update. When people receive a memo or note, there is a logical progression of questions to flood their mind: *What is this? What is the importance of this message (to me)? In light of this information, now what am I supposed to think, feel, do?* Given that this is the natural expectation of the receiver of your message, it is on you, the messenger, to appropriately frame the message. Describe the situation simply (*what*), make sense of the facts and identify implications (*so what*), and define a course of action (*now what*). In this case, we must tell people *what, so what,* and *now what.* Here are two examples of how to do this. The first is a longer, friendlier tone; the second is faster and more direct. Both work, so choose whichever approach best suits your goal and audience.

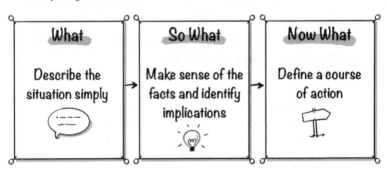

Here's an example of a *what, so what, now what* email in a longer/ friendlier tone:

Hi Product Teams,

Hope your week has been great. I am writing to let you know that initial onboarding with small media content has proven successful. So the content manager team will continue onboarding major content in the upcoming quarters. *(what)*

This is exciting because these are major steps toward moving all the media stack to native, which will mean additional performance improvement as we become one platform. *(so what)*

We want this to be a collaborative and seamless process for all involved. Toward that effort, I will be reaching out to individual team leads as we get ready for your onboarding. While we are fully aware that priorities may shift, attached to this email is an overview of our proposed timeline. *(now what)*

I welcome your feedback and questions!

Wishing you a wonderful weekend, Trey

Here's an example draft of a *what, so what, now what* email using a short/direct tone:

Product Teams,

Initial onboarding has gone well. We will continue to onboard major content in the upcoming quarters. *(what)*

These are critical steps to ensuring better performance as we become one platform. *(so what)*

Below is an overview of our current timeline. *(now what)*

—Trey

In each of these examples, the idea is that you will put forth the effort of making the message make sense for your audience. Your ability to structure your message with a simple, logical flow is not only a benefit to your audience, but it is also an opportunity to promote yourself as an effective communicator—someone people can trust and rely on to convey meaning and accomplish communication goals. If I trust you in my inbox, I am more inclined to believe that I can trust you to meet with clients, present to the executive leadership team, and so on.

ESSENTIAL TAKEAWAYS

- Don't dilute the impact of your words or sabotage yourself with sloppy and unnecessary emails or messaging.

- Don't data-dump or expect after-hour responses unless that expectation is established in advance.

- If you wouldn't feel comfortable cc'ing your local news reporter and county sheriff on your email, think twice before sending it.

- If you want people to avoid misunderstandings and remember specific decisions made during a meeting, take the extra step of sending a recap message.

- When writing emails, follow one of two easy frameworks: *recap, request, remind* or *what, so what, now what.*

CHAPTER

15

Communicate to Make and Maintain Social Relationships

The previous chapters covered how to communicate your way into a job (Chapter 12) and up the career ladder (Chapter 13). Along the way, however, there will be any number of opportunities to make and maintain relationships, which might elevate your experience in your role or help you establish that next great opportunity. In this chapter, I focus on how communication essentials, specifically friendship work, can help you maintain a robust network that will help you have a more satisfying career. Big picture: Friendship work[1] is about employing communication strategies that help you form and maintain meaningful connections with others; it is more fun than homework, and the benefits are aplenty.

To get started, let's consider my client, Jerry. When we first met, Jerry had already earned his PhD and was working toward an MBA. He had achieved great things, yet he saw zero upward mobility in his current role and was eager to leverage his MBA to make a career change. To my surprise, he had no professional network to leverage in his attempt to make a professional transition. So, he was relying on recruitment events and information sessions being hosted by firms recruiting candidates like him. His major stress: How do I talk to these people when I get there?

This is a normal stressor for most job seekers, and it is pretty similar to the stress that people feel when trying to meet potential dating partners. In my experience as a communication coach, I have found that most people find day-to-day interactions with others to be pretty easy, until they are trying to achieve a professional or relational goal, like getting a job or a date. I asked Jerry how he would walk up to and start a conversation with people at a professional conference. Blank stare. I asked Jerry how he would manage a lunch conversation with new colleagues or how he might introduce himself at a neighborhood gathering. Blank stare. We talked and figured out a game plan, but the bottom line was that Jerry needed a professional network and wanted friends, both of which he didn't have much of.

I know that feeling of wanting something and thinking about it, but failing to achieve it. For the past two years, I have thought and thought about having a vegetable garden in my backyard. Guess what I grew during that time? Nothing! Turns out that merely thinking about wanting a garden doesn't do much good. Finally, my family and I decided to go outside and prepare the ground, buy the seeds, plant them, and do the work. Now we are incorporating fresh produce from our backyard into nearly every dinner.

Human interaction and relationships can be a bit like gardening. When people go off to college or move to a new city for work, they often talk about the need to build a network and meet people. Some may even bemoan not knowing anyone or lament their dating prospects. But their relationship situation will be like my garden—just a thought until they get out there and do the work.

The truth is we need relationships, and communication is how we form and maintain those relationships. Whether they are personal or professional, relationships require communication skills in action, much like having a garden requires actual gardening. And just like fresh produce sustains you, the benefits of a robust professional network, friendships, and social relationships are endless.

Relationships are formed through communication

DO YOUR FRIENDSHIP WORK

As the pandemic rattled our society, we became reminded of the importance of friendships and social relationships. Even beyond factors related to the actual illness, some specific residual matters related to human communication stood out to me as I worked with my students and clients. Perhaps most notably is that no matter how people felt about the change of work, nearly all my clients mentioned feeling sad or lonely on account of missing connections with their colleagues, friends, and social network. Even though some managed to be creative by hosting virtual happy hours or watch parties, most people significantly grieved the lack of social connectedness.

Aside from a self-imposed choice to go on a silent retreat of sorts, I wonder how long you or I could be completely isolated from others, especially our chosen and preferred friends, before suffering from the negative effects of isolation. Even this pales in comparison to challenges experienced by those in solitary confinement, military deployment, or nursing home loneliness. Many of my clients live lives that most of the world would envy, yet during the pandemic they lacked the ability to see their friends as usual, and this was what grieved them. During the height of the pandemic, I received calls from clients who just wanted to talk. They said things like, "I am so accustomed to traveling for work and being on client sites, I feel kind of depressed just being cooped up, taking virtual calls from my apartment all day." Their distress highlights the importance of making and maintaining friends and social relationships, because, even when all else is good in your world, the quality of your personal relationships is what matters most.

Each of us is born with a drive to seek, form, maintain, and protect strong relationships. We may not always know how or choose to put forth the effort, but instinctually we are wired for meaningful human connection. In addition to the material benefits of friendship (such as having someone to help you unpack your moving van), close and satisfying relationships bring us unparalleled emotional and health benefits. Whom do you call in the middle of a workday for a good laugh, to vent a little, or to get a word of encouragement? I'm guessing you picked a friend or family member who feels like a friend. These interactions with close others are an emotional uplift, and they also ward off some of the negative effects of stress that may cause a long list of health concerns, like sleep problems, heart disease, and depression.[2] The research on how close and satisfying social relationships benefit our lives is extensive, which helps to explain why people who never experienced the actual wrath of the coronavirus in their own home still felt the pain of the pandemic.

Given all of this, it seems that a major life priority for anyone would be to do the friendship work necessary for making and maintaining close and satisfying friendships and social relationships. And even if you are less inclined to expand your Friday night Supper Club, all ambitious professionals should be doing the work to advance and nurture their professional networks. Either way, you are in luck because we are about to address how to do both.

REAP THE RELATIONAL HARVEST

Like my garden, social relationships don't just develop out of thin air. Fortunately, there are essential communication skills you can use to form and nurture them. For our purposes, I focus on face-to-face interaction. It is well known that physical proximity is a critical factor for making friendships, as you are more likely to make friends with someone who works in your hallway or lives in your building. This is for a few reasons. Namely, the convenience of bumping into one another, followed by the likelihood of some shared commonality and probable talking points. In addition, here are some communication skills you should use when forming connections with others.

Extend Invitations

Those skilled in initiating relationships know how to approach others, strike up a conversation, and make good first impressions (discussed in detail in Chapter 13). The simple formula is to be likeable, extend invitations when appropriate, and see what happens.

As an example, I recently had new neighbors move in next door. I didn't pop up on their doorstep and barge in for a tour of their house. That might have screamed stranger-danger. Instead, I allowed a little time to pass, and when we both happened to be outside, I waved and sought an opportunity to strike up a conversation. I didn't talk about myself; instead, I engaged in ways that invited him to share whatever he was open to sharing. I looked for areas of commonality that I could build on in future interactions. We both have kids. We both like to run. I then gave him my phone number, letting him know to count me in should he want to go for a run or walk our kids to the nearby playground. Simple as that.

And the same can be true of forming relationships in the workplace. If a new leader is named at your organization, don't fight to be first on her calendar. Instead, look for a natural opportunity to meet. Don't spout off your grievances or requests, invite her to share how her week is going and what the transition has been like. Look for areas of commonality that you can build upon for future interactions. Simple as that.

In my earlier example with my client Jerry, I encouraged him to imagine people at information sessions like books he had never read before. Instead of entering conversations with the sole intention of reciting your life story and all of your credentials to others, consider what you might gain from taking interest in *their* stories and what they have to say. Many career-motivated people walk up to recruiters, hiring managers, and decision makers immediately talking about themselves and trying to impose their value proposition, but imagine how beneficial it would be to interact with others in the spirit of friendship, by focusing not on *you* but on *the other person*. For example:

> "Hi, I'm Trey. Thank you so much for hosting this event tonight. My peers and I are all so glad for the chance to meet people from your firm. How long have you been with the company? . . . Oh, really, four years! I imagine you've had an incredible four years, especially given the unique challenges and opportunities during the pandemic. . . . So, what did life look like before joining the firm? . . . Oh, wow, you lived in the Bay Area? How cool. I'm planning a trip there in the fall. Any must-try restaurants or recommendations?" *(Conversation ensues.)*
>
> "Look, I know you have plenty of other people to connect with tonight. Thanks for giving me a few minutes to visit and get to know you. I can tell your firm is an incredible place with some wonderful people, and I'd love to have a coffee chat soon to learn more. What is the best way to stay connected?"

People crave connection that is enjoyable and, at a minimum, equitable. Social exchange theory argues that people seek to form and maintain relationships in which the benefits outweigh the costs.[3] The idea here is that we don't want to get the raw end of a deal. In the workplace, it doesn't feel good to be taken advantage of by a colleague. If a colleague always asked you to cover for him or her but was seldom available to cover for you, then that would be an unequal social exchange. In that instance, you would be "under-benefited" and your colleague would be "over-benefited" by this exchange. In most cases, the ideal is that both colleagues perceive a sense of equity,[4] such that both feel like the amount of support received from a colleague is equal to the amount given. At minimum, we know that people don't want to be under-benefited. Nobody wants to be the one always picking up the slack and buying lunch, right? Sadly, most job seekers and career-hungry persons are far too focused on talking about themselves and asking for favors. They forget the importance of playing by friendship rules, and therefore nearly every client I work with is flabbergasted when I model for them what good professional networking looks like. The truth is that good networking is not all that different from being a good neighbor. Quality networking is about taking sincere interest in the other person and looking for areas of genuine commonality, rather than expecting someone to stand by and listening to a run-through of your life story and value proposition. Otherwise, when you extend that invitation and ask for coffee, the person on the other end will either reject it or regret saying yes, unwilling to waste more time hearing about you and how great you think you are.

In short, one way to ensure a strong start in your personal and professional relationships is to remember that people are more likely to seek a second encounter when they felt the first interaction was equitable and enjoyable.

Be a Positive and Supportive Communicator

Simply put, a critical component of nurturing a personal or professional relationship is to be courteous and refrain from unnecessary criticism. Being positive means smiling sincerely and frequently, expressing appreciation, and not complaining. Doing these things makes us likeable and causes others to feel comfortable around us. To test yourself and gauge the amount of positivity you communicate, ask yourself questions like these:

- Do you find positive topics of conversation to focus on?

- Do you express joy for others' good news?

- Do you enjoy laughing and sharing uplifting humor with others?[5]

I encourage you to avoid the pitfalls of negativity at work for two key reasons. First, consider that most jobs have a life span, much like a vehicle has a life span. The sooner you go negative, the sooner you are diminishing the life span of your job. When we go negative at work in our thoughts, words, or actions, it is like slamming brakes, burning rubber, or skipping oil changes. If you go negative and trash your job or your car, you shouldn't be surprised when you have that itching feeling to trade it in.

Second, the sooner you go negative, the sooner you are branding yourself as a difficult person. It's hard for people to like, advocate for, and promote a person that they perceive to be negative or difficult. A word to the wise: avoid going negative or being associated with negative others. And if you must interact with a negative person at work, play dumb to that person's negative humor with comments like, "Oh, really, I hadn't noticed. Good to know. Thanks for the heads-up. See you later." You don't increase your brand value by knowing the dirt and calling it out.

And if a professional relationship requires you to communicate negatively or like a "downer," you are better off ignoring the water-cooler gossip and picking happier people to network with. Establishing ties with negative individuals won't pay out in the end because those ties could potentially (re)brand you in a negative light and may diminish the life span of your job satisfaction.

Once you know you are networking with positive people, begin layering those relationships with supportive assurances to illustrate your goodwill and intent to nurture the friendship. For example, suppose the new neighbor and I have been on a run or taken our kids to the park, and I trust him to be a quality guy that I wish to stay connected with. Then if he later asks me to drive him to the airport, I could affirm with, "OK, what time?" Or I can utilize this as a chance to provide what is called a relationship assurance by saying something like, "Gladly, you are my neighbor and friend. What time should I get you?"

There is no benefit to overdoing it and saluting or taking a blood oath. The idea is that through subtle yet supportive and assuring messages, you affirm to the other that the relationship is important to you. If this were a colleague, you send this message: "Enjoyed grabbing lunch last week and learning about some of the cool projects you are managing right now. Hope to do it again soon." Don't overcomplicate it. But if you want to be intentional about expanding your personal or professional network, that starts with extending invitations and being a positive, assuring, and supportive communicator.

Forming a social relationship doesn't necessarily imply a desire to maintain it for the long haul. There are many reasons a social relationship may end. For instance, certain events can cause friends to dislike each other (e.g., Greg takes credit for Alfredo's work). Likewise, changes in life circumstances may decrease opportunities for communication (e.g., Cassie moved out of Lauren's neighborhood; Mallory was transferred out of Shannon's working team). You can likely recall a friendship that started strong but faded over time—perhaps a neighbor you no longer pop in on or a colleague you no longer have lunch with. In most cases, the work of maintaining the relationship no longer felt beneficial. Relationships carry costs as well as rewards. The neighbor needing your sugar but never sharing in return or the colleague who is always relying on you for help but is never available to bail you out—

both are creating unequitable relationships that you will likely choose to back away from.

Some of these situations may not always be fun or enjoyable to navigate. But unless you have a strong reason for cutting someone off cold, your best option is to draw your boundary lines while wearing a smile, remaining a positive and encouraging—albeit unavailable—individual.

ESSENTIAL TAKEAWAYS

- Imagine how beneficial it would be to interact with others if you focused not on *you* but on *the other person*.

- People are more likely to seek a second encounter when they felt the first interaction was equitable and enjoyable.

- Be courteous and refrain from unnecessary criticism. Being positive means smiling sincerely, frequently expressing appreciation, and not complaining.

- Don't allow yourself to be drawn into negative relationships at work; they will diminish your personal brand and not serve you well in the long term.

Communicate Through Conflict and Difficult Conversations

The previous chapter focused on how we utilize essential communication skills to make and maintain meaningful relationships at work and beyond. The upside of these connections is endless, but with each relationship comes the possibility of conflict and the probability of difficult conversations along the way. This, unto itself, is not a bad thing, but many people lack the willingness or ability to manage these interactions effectively. Some even struggle with knowing how to talk about conflict and difficult conversations after the fact.

If you are like most of my clients, you will agree that two of the most dreaded interview questions are "Tell me about how you handled a workplace conflict" and "Tell me about a time that you received (or gave) difficult feedback." These interview questions reveal that organizations understand how problematic and challenging workplace interactions can be, especially if they are not managed well.

As a quick aside, when you are preparing your responses to such questions, it is critically important that you focus on how difficult and challenging situations can bring about positive outcomes. How were you able to harness conflict for good? How were you able to take difficult feedback and use it as fuel for professional development? But interview preparation aside, it is really important to know how you should communicate through difficult conversations and conflict because they are inevitable.

WHAT CONSTITUTES CONFLICT?

First, it is important that you recognize that interpersonal conflict is uniquely different from simply being irritated by or disappointed in someone. On many occasions, I have had a client tell me about a conflict at work that isn't actually a conflict. You can feel all the frustration and anger in the world and still not necessarily have a conflict with someone.

For there to be conflict, there must be an expressed struggle between at least two interdependent parties who perceive incompatible goals, scarce resources, and interference from the other party in achieving their goals.[1] If the struggle is not shared, it isn't a conflict. For example, if my favorite singer behaves in a reprehensible way, I might be disappointed or even disgusted, but there is no conflict to manage because there is no relationship between us. Similarly, if your CEO announces a particular policy that you disagree with, there is no potential conflict until you express disagreement. If your CEO doesn't know you exist, your disagreement isn't likely to become an interpersonal conflict, because your relationship is not—and is unlikely to become—interdependent.

In a more likely scenario, you may find it frustrating that your manager never asks for your opinion or viewpoint during weekly meetings, but the conflict is only in your head until you express it. With that in mind, I suggest you address it early and positively. An example would be:

> "Hey Trey, I'd love a chance to provide some inputs and updates during future meetings. I want the team to know that I am actively invested in the project. Can we find a slot in the next meeting for me to share about X?"

Taking the frustration out of it and seeing the situation as a positive opportunity increases the likelihood that you will get what you want. It could also potentially prevent future conflict. The alternative may be that your frustration grows over time, you assume the worst in your manager, and you take it out on him or her during a future one-to-one meeting.

Conflict is about the *perception* of incompatible goals and scarce resources. If you sit in budget meetings, work cross-functionally, or find yourself negotiating with others for space or headcount, then you already understand how quickly conversations around resource allocation can escalate. I like to remind my clients that, when possible, it is best to pull back, listen to all sides, find the commonality, and steer conversation toward shared values. Take this example of administrators discussing where they'd like to allocate the university's attention and resources:

> **One administrator declares:** "There is only one issue to address, and it's student retention. Without enough students on campus, our doors will close!"

> **Another administrator quickly declares:** "Enough talking about retention. We can't just snap our fingers or buy our way out of that. But we can create more parking spaces. People

shouldn't have to drive in circles for hours searching for a spot. Let's spend the money and finally fix the parking problem."

This perception of incompatible goals and scarce resources argued in this way elevates the threat of conflict and leads people to believe that one side must lose for the other to win.

To be a savvy communicator in this situation, however, you should try to find the complementary overlap and focus your message accordingly:

> "I appreciate the opportunity to hear both viewpoints. I agree that parking is rough and needs improvement. I also agree that doing our part to increase student retention is a responsibility we each bear. As I did some listening and digging, I learned that one of our most frequently cited complaints by students leaving the university is their frustration with parking. In other words, it appears that everyone in this room is correct in their thinking. We seem to be looking at the same coin, just from different sides. By allocating a portion of our resources toward improved parking, something we can do immediately, we are in fact addressing our most critical concern—retention."

As with all my examples, I want you to focus on style and tone rather than evaluating these messages word by word. This tactic—of demonstrating active listening, reflecting, and maintaining your focus on what is universally shared—can help to establish commonality, minimize the perception of incompatible goals, and thereby minimize or alleviate the conflict. If someone bristles and immediately rebuts with more points of disagreement, sincerely thank them for the input, assure them they have been heard, and state the case that you would like to first focus on those points that are agreed on.

GAIN CONSENSUS FOR THE PROBLEM BEFORE FOCUSING ON THE SOLUTION

In some cases, it will be nearly impossible for people to agree on the solution if they aren't looking at the same problem.[2] An interactive map can't accurately tell you which way to turn if it doesn't know precisely where you are and what you are facing. And you can't answer "4" until I show you the flashcard that says "2 + 2." If only business problems were so easy!

The trouble becomes that when leading a project or driving a meeting, it is easy to already have the right answer in your mind. So many people will draft a memo or hold the conversation hyperfocused on getting consensus about next steps and how to do them, failing to identify and establish consensus on the problem being solved. To increase the likelihood that people will agree on the solution, it's worth taking a few minutes to ensure everyone is in agreement about what the problem is and how important it is to solve it.

The next time you find yourself in a meeting that seems to be going nowhere good and people are bickering over solutions, here are a few simple things to try. For starters, you can ask that people take a minute to revisit the problem statement with a comment like this:

> "I am hearing some interesting ideas from across the group. As we continue to consider these ideas, I want to make sure we have the right criteria for evaluating them. Coming into this meeting, I understood that our objective was x. Is that everyone else's understanding?"

If the response is not affirmative, the next step is to acknowledge the obvious:

"It's clear that we are not completely aligned on our problem statement. Before we continue trying to propose and evaluate a potential solution, I encourage us to get some clarity on what the actual problem is that we are trying to solve."

Once the response is affirmative and there is consensus on the problem, I urge you to write it on the board or type it into the chat with the heading, "Problem statement." With the problem stated and agreed on, you can now move forward on some solid ground. The added step of writing the problem statement for all to see is critical. This way, if someone attempts to veer off from the problem at hand, anyone can choose to point to the board and say, "Well, it's a cool idea, but it doesn't help us solve for x."

These tips are very effective in small groups and work teams, but you can also use them in one-on-one meetings, especially when meeting with someone who tends to steamroll conversation. If you feel funny telling people that you are going to write out the problem statement, you can just chalk it up as doing a favor for you and others who are visually oriented. These communication essentials around conflict mitigation help to save time, prevent unnecessary gridlock, and may spare some bruised egos.

For example, as I write this, I'm recalling a recent situation where my client was on a call with his sales team and their new second-line sales leader hopped on just to take part in the call. The entire team had reached consensus on the problem and was aligned on how to move forward, but the new boss felt the need to be present and flex some muscle, and he ended up flooding the meeting with unrelated ideas he had heard in senior leader meetings. The problem is that the sales team was down to the wire on closing this big deal. The team just needed a green light—and fast—from the new boss on some additional funding for a "no-brainer" statement of work that would yield much-needed new revenue.

Torn between not usurping the new boss while also securing the statement of work for his team, my client decided to message his boss a quick note saying, *Please, trust me on this one.* He then proceeded to publicly thank his boss for providing a "fresh set of eyes" on the situation, highlighting that it was "beneficial to have insight into conversations happening among leadership." He then refocused everyone's attention to the problem at hand and asked how soon they could expect a green light. The boss responded, "I've got confidence in you all. Sounds like you know what the best path forward is. Consider it a green light. Let's lock it up."

The essential takeaway from my client is that he knew that to win on one front meant he must win on all fronts. It was critical that he protect the boss's ego by communicating respect and appreciation for his input before refocusing everyone's attention to the problem statement and, ultimately, making his request for the green light.

AVOID CONFLICT WITHOUT AVOIDING ISSUES

When facing a heavy issue or potentially difficult conversation, my clients often mention wishing they could avoid it altogether. And although it's admirable to avoid conflict, avoiding the issues themselves is problematic. When someone is failing to meet deadlines, underperforming, or otherwise missing the mark, those situations need to be addressed. When someone's attitude or behavior is wrecking the morale of the team and compromising workplace culture, that also needs to be addressed.

Unless you enjoy conflict, your goal should be to navigate the issue and influence a positive change without causing any unnecessary conflict. To do this, you must imagine that the person or people with whom you have potential conflict are not your adversaries. They are not on the opposing side of your tennis court. Instead, you must visualize yourself walking to the other side of the net or inviting them to your side of the net. You need to view *your* want or need through *the other person's* perspective and translated into their language.

For example, you manage Jed. He's a good guy, but he struggles with taking on too much work and then he misses important deadlines here and there. Anytime someone nags him about a deadline in a team meeting, he acts surprised. You've tried nudging him gently about keeping up with deadlines, but it's not working and he's acting defeated. He has potential to really thrive in his role, but because he is on rocky ground with deadlines, his colleagues are getting frustrated. How do you nudge him without nagging? How do you address the issue head-on while avoiding an unnecessary conflict?

There is no magic wand to wave, but your best bet is to partner with Jed. You must avoid any temptation to see Jed as your opposition. He is not your enemy or your problem. *Missing deadlines* is your shared problem. To partner with Jed in solving the problem, you must describe the problem through a shared perspective. In other words, get on the same side of the court, so that you are scoring points together, not against one another.

You might schedule a one-on-one and your message would be something like:

> "Jed, you have great potential to thrive in your role. I've known that and believed it fully ever since our last evaluation together, when you shared that your goal was to get promoted by the

end of the year. Since then, I've seen that you've been raising your hand for extra work, and I applaud that. The problem, as best I can tell, is that all that extra work seems to be compromising your turnaround time on some of the more important work. And this problem is compromising your larger goal of getting promoted.

"As your manager, I want to see you thrive. I want to see you reach your goal. At the end of the year, I want to be completing your evaluation and bragging about your ability to hit deadlines and impress your colleagues. We aren't there right now, but I believe we can be. Let's come up with a plan for how best to move forward."

In this example, everything is honest and sincere. Jed is not your problem. And therefore you don't need to become his problem. You can stay on the same team with a shared commitment to overcoming obstacles that prevent you from achieving mutually agreed on goals and objectives. This extra step in how to work with people best allows you to strengthen your professional bonds while tackling issues and avoiding unnecessary conflict.

HARNESS CONFLICT FOR GOOD

At times, conflict is inevitable and can actually be beneficial. Working through conflict in a positive, constructive manner can help two people learn more about each other and their relationship.

For example, my friend tells the story of his first inside-sales job, where he had to share cubicle space with a guy he liked—they had a lot in common and even liked to skip out early to hit golf balls on occasion. But this guy also nearly drove my friend mad! Their cubicles were shaped so they faced each other with a thin hallway between them. My friend was growing increasingly frustrated with his cubicle buddy, mostly because he snacked for hours on end throughout the day. The sight, sound, and occasional smells of his endless snacking were getting under my friend's skin.

When I asked him how he handled this situation, my friend shared that after a restless night of thinking about how frustrated the snacking was making him and that he couldn't stand another day of it, he decided to text his friend a note first thing in the morning that read, *Hey, I need to talk about something when you have a minute. It might be awkward, please hear me out.* When they finally chatted, it turned out the frustration was going both ways. While my friend was put out by the endless snacking, his colleague had a few requests of his own. He requested that my friend please stop streaming videos unless he was wearing headphones, and that he avoid bringing in loud office guests unless he was actually getting work done.

That was more than a decade ago, and they have stayed great friends. Had they never addressed their frustrations and confronted the elephant in the cubicle, they would have never developed the close relationship they have today.

In the case of my friend and his colleague, they were able to bring their frustrations to the forefront in a way that led to better outcomes for them individually, and in the process they discovered how much they each valued the other, which meant a greater sense of closeness as colleagues and friends. Managing difficult conversations well, as they did, is how people can harness potential conflict for something good.

Conversely, when individuals are triggered by potential conflict and choose to *avoid* (e.g., ghost the person until we assume frustrations have subsided) or *compete* (e.g., win at all costs, by convincing the other that he or she is wrong and that you and your ideas are not to be questioned), the closeness and satisfaction of the relationship will suffer. Instead, by approaching potential conflict with a collaborative and compromising mindset, people can harness the conflict for good, often leading to higher-quality outcomes and stronger bonds.

In fact, there is a great deal of research to support the notion that conflict is not itself bad or damaging to relationships; instead, it's how people manage the conflict that matters. Psychologist John Gottman has spent decades studying how relationship partners interact with one another during conflict and the impact these interactions have on the longevity of the relationship.[3] Often considered in the context of marital relationships, the wisdom from Gottman's research can be applied broadly, to include personal and professional relationships.

There are four specific communication behaviors, which become particularly amplified when one of the interactants is prone to behaving with narcissistic, impulsive, or manipulative tendencies.[4] Gottman calls these destructive conflict behaviors the "Four Horsemen": criticism, defensiveness, contempt, and stonewalling. By identifying them, we are better able to spot them as they happen and hopefully eliminate and replace them with healthy, productive communication. Let's take a closer look at each of these behaviors.

How to Handle Criticism

Criticizing someone is not the same as offering a substantive complaint or critique. To criticize is to attack the core of a person's character. Consider the difference of the same issue between criticizing your colleague and expressing a complaint. For example, an unhealthy criticism may sound like this:

"You never think about how your actions affect the rest of the team. You didn't just forget to call, you were being selfish!"

In contrast, a reasonable complaint may sound like this:

"I was concerned when you were running late to the client meeting and didn't text me. I thought we had agreed to always check in and give a heads-up."

If you find yourself prone to thinking critical thoughts, you are in good company. The first of the Four Horsemen (i.e., criticism) is very common (especially in romantic relationships). The solution is to train yourself to convert critical thoughts into legitimate and well-formulated complaints. You will know you have done this well if your message focuses on a specific event and how it made you feel, rather than a broad and global statement that attacks someone else's character.

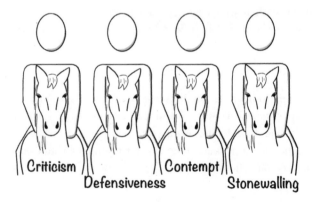

The Four Horsemen

Criticism
Defensiveness
Contempt
Stonewalling

How to Handle Defensiveness

A typical response to criticism is the equally destructive act of being defensive. Most everyone can relate to defensiveness, as it is the knee-jerk reaction to feeling unjustly accused. Instinctually, people will behave defensively by fishing for excuses and playing the innocent victim, sometimes to simply get someone off their backs. Imagine a scenario where your colleague asks:

"Did you let the accounts team know we weren't joining the sync-up this afternoon?"

A defensive response might be:

"I was just too busy, I figured you would know that. Why didn't you just do it?"

A nondefensive response is one that accepts responsibility and understands the other's perspective. It may sound like this:

"I dropped the ball on that. I should have asked you this morning to do it because I knew my day would be packed. That's my fault. Let me call them right now."

No matter how you may justify your defensive message, the result will always lead to escalating the conflict. Even playing the innocent victim (e.g., "Well, boss, I just don't understand why you are picking on me. Don't I do a lot of good work? It feels like there is no way to win around here.") is a defensive posture leading to a no-win situation.

If you feel the issue must be addressed, it is better to start with how you feel and ask for advice on how to move forward—for example:

> "I am feeling frustrated. From best I can tell, I am doing good work that is not seen. I need your advice on how to fix things around here."

Whereas a defensive posture is sure to betray your executive presence, a vulnerable position that starts with how you are feeling and ends with what you need has a higher probability of gaining respect and leading to better outcomes.

How to Handle Contempt

While the negative behavior of criticizing attacks character, the unhealthy act of contempt assumes a moral superiority over another person. Imagine a colleague or partner who says:

> "Seriously, stop walking around acting so tired. You have no clue the day I've had. Meetings galore and with no end in sight. I have been running a hundred miles an hour, and you walk in here all just to plop down on the chair. Get a clue."

Contempt comes from built-up negative thoughts about your colleague or partner. Imagine how a comment like "You sure look tired. Better get used to this pace of work" eventually becomes the previous comment.

If you are thinking contemptuous comments, you need to take five minutes and clear your head before speaking such venom. Communicating contempt never helps you or anyone else. If you are on the receiving end of contemptuous comments in the workplace, you can start with reflecting back to the speaker that you are feeling uncomfortable and request a time-out (e.g., "Hey, I'm not feeling very good about this conversation. In fact, it's making me kind of uncomfortable. Is there any way we could try to have this conversation later?"). Additionally, it may be wise to document such instances and seek the advice of a trusted leader or appropriate resource within your organization.

How to Handle Stonewalling

Where one person's criticism or contempt usually causes the other to get defensive, eventually one person is likely to stonewall, which is a form of evasiveness. Stonewalling is that tendency people have to shut down or act too busy to even notice the other person. In remote work or digital communication, this may look like not responding to a person's message or other forms of ghosting. I have a client who tells me that one of his direct reports is so upset with him that when they are on a virtual team call, she will turn her camera off every time he is talking and turn it back on when someone else is speaking. It's her way of sending a message of stonewalling in a virtual environment.

When colleagues or partners begin to show contempt or stonewall, a tragic conflict cycle is underway. For those of us wishing to stay gainfully and joyfully employed, it is wise to break the cycle. There is the adage that "when they go low, we go high." Stonewalling is going low. If someone you work with is going low, try going high with a vulnerable message, such as:

> "Look, I care about you, and I care about our ability to do great work together. I see that there is a distance between us and our ability to communicate effectively. I'm willing to do my part, but I need some input from you. What do you believe can be done to help us turn a corner and try to communicate better?"

This might not work, but at least you will know that you took the high road and did your part.

Take Five to Consider Your Response Before Saying Something You'll Regret

By now, it must be clear that managing conflict is not easy. Breaking conflict cycles is especially hard to do because we are creatures of habit. It requires a lot of maturity, digging deep, often letting go of ego, and communicating with intentionality.

For example, one of my clients is a senior vice president at a successful Silicon Valley startup, who has been with his company since it started and is highly invested in his work. The job is high pressure, with long hours, and the work environment is extremely competitive. Across the organization, people politic for more visibility and decision-making power. My client and I had developed systems for navigating his workplace dynamics. He was doing perfectly fine until one day, unbeknownst to him, the CEO hired a counterpart who would share certain responsibilities with my client. I could see that my client was growing more anxious and tense as he and his new colleague jockeyed for corporate muscle. So we started meeting much more regularly to ensure he was showing up to work with the right mindset and messaging.

But that wasn't enough. The conflict with his new counterpart was negatively impacting his thoughts, damaging his confidence, and adversely impacting his ability to communicate effectively with others at work. He was starting to blurt out negative comments in meetings. Traditionally someone who is calm, cool, collected, and assured of himself, he started to resemble someone lost in an ocean. He was so focused on only the water immediately surrounding him that he was losing sight of a bigger picture or the fact that if he stopped treading the conflict water he could just stand up on his own feet and walk to shore.

Don't get so caught up on what's right in front of you that you forget the bigger picture

In heated situations, he needed to be thinking beyond the immediate moment he was in. He needed to get his eyes above the waves. I told him about a technique, take five, that I use and encourage others to try as well. To take five is to ask for a five-minute break to use the restroom, get a coffee, or fill your water bottle. In those five minutes (or even a minute or two if you can't get away for five minutes), think of how you want to remember this moment in five hours. Then ask yourself how you would like to remember this moment in five days, five months, or five years from now. Do you want to remember childish behavior? (I hope not.) Do you want to remember saying something you regret now? (Again, I hope not.) Do you want to remember taking the high road? (I hope so!) You can intervene and potentially influence your own conflict positively by taking a small step back and considering how you want to move forward on a smoother path.

When you take five, you can start avoiding conflict traps. In fact, you can begin to turn potential conflict into reasons for feeling closer and more connected. Imagine a colleague or friend shoots you a text like this:

Hey, I'm bummed you bailed on that meetup last night. I only went because you said you were going. What happened?

You could act sensitive or be defensive, or you could harness the potential conflict for something good by replying:

You are right to call me out. I should have been there. I got caught at the office and failed to check the time before it was too late. I never intended to let you down. I hope you forgive me. I won't let that happen again!

The alternative would be to ignore (i.e., stonewalling; ghosting) or refute the message of vulnerability (i.e., defensiveness; denial). In most cases, your better alternative is to own the blame and turn the negative into a positive reinforcement.

By knowing the Four Horsemen of conflict and how certain personality types, like narcissistic or manipulative tendencies, can take them from a gallop to a sprint, you can more easily identify them and actively work to eliminate them. It's even more important to replace the Four Horsemen with more effective communication techniques. The take five concept is actually something you can try using with a trusted other. If you have someone in your organization whom you trust to have your back and protect your best interest, I encourage you to ask that person to message you a signal (e.g., *Trust me. Take five.*) if you are ever in a meeting and appear as though you might say or do something regrettable. Following this advice, some of my clients in high-pressure roles have found take five accountability buddies at work, and they tell me this approach works great! Practicing these communication essentials has high potential for protecting your personal and professional relationships.

DISAGREE AND COMMIT
(OR STEP ASIDE)

While there may be good reason to hold your tongue on occasion, there is also a time and place to break from popular opinion and express your disagreement. Legendary companies like Intel and Amazon have long instituted leadership principles about the importance of demonstrating the courage and ability to appropriately and effectively speak up and share your point of view, even if it is unpopular and especially when doing so protects the interest of the organization.[5] At Amazon, it is not enough to agree to disagree. The leadership principle advises that people disagree and commit.[6] To do this means voicing a well-developed viewpoint passionately; however, once a leader has decided on the best path forward, you must get on board and commit to the decision (even if it isn't yours!).

If you work in an environment that adheres to similar principles like disagree and commit, here are three pointers to remember. First, have a smart point of view and share it openly during the dedicated discussion time. Second, demonstrate conviction and be willing to put your cards on the table, share your best ideas, and disagree, if necessary. Third, no matter the outcome, even if your point of view is overruled, suck it up, put your smile on, and commit to the decision that has been made.

These steps are easier said than done. First of all, to have a well-developed point of view requires that you be highly invested in the topic at hand, and to voice your point of view can feel very vulnerable. Then, once you've invested your energies toward establishing a point of view and put yourself in a vulnerable position to share it aloud— even though it may likely be rejected or overruled—you must then suck it up and show some team spirit.

No matter your age or rank, following the principle of disagree and commit is not for the weak. Imagine a family of four is deciding between a day at the lake or a day at the beach. If two choose the lake and two choose the beach, but ultimately a ranking member of the family calls the shot and picks the lake, should the two who advocated for the beach whine the entire day at the lake or commit wholly to making it the best trip possible? It may seem obvious that they should be excited about going to the lake (as a dad, I can even picture myself thinking, *Hey, we should all just be grateful we are going on a fun trip anywhere.*), but consider that some may have wholeheartedly believed their point of view was the right one and then they got overruled.

Rank and seniority aside, consider a work team of four consultants deciding on a layout for their slide deck that will be presented to the executive team. If one person differs during the discussion period, how should the one who disagreed show up on presentation day? I certainly hope he wouldn't spend the presentation rolling his eyes at the slide deck and drawing attention to all the things he would have done differently. No, we expect him to shake off the disagreement and commit wholly to the success of the team.

We can and maybe even should expect that from him, but reasonable expectations alone don't make it easier for the one who got overruled. When applying the principle of disagree and commit, I encourage my clients to visualize themselves as a member of a basketball team; a time-out has been called and the players are huddled up and trying to make a play call. Even if three of the five players disagree on the play that was called, they'd better all execute the play to perfection if they wish to be successful. Communicators who are striving for success must adopt a commit mindset, even in the face of disagreement. I believe you will find that, although difficult, adopting this mindset helps to ensure disagreements don't necessitate conflict.

Unfortunately, though, this is not always the case at home or at work. Many people behave and communicate from an "agree to disagree" mentality, which if you think about it often sounds like, "I am right and you are wrong, and in time you will figure that out." Imagine what would happen if the team preparing its presentation to the senior executives took an agree to disagree attitude. Some would roll their eyes and let their presentation fail. Beyond the obvious failure this would end in, what would that do to trust on their team? In the absence of trust, what good is the team at all? Avoid this mindset like the plague. Such a posture draws a proverbial line in the sand and emboldens some people to root against their own family and coworkers.

Even in disagreement or conflict, adopting communication essentials can help you to behave and communicate better. We can be people who have difficult conversations, disagreements even, but still commit to the people and the success of the group. Doing so is how savvy communicators protect their personal and professional relationships, which are essential for living a successful and satisfying life.

SAY GOODBYE WELL

All jobs come to an end. This is inevitable. If lucky, you have the opportunity to manage your exit and ensure that you say goodbye well. Chapter 13 discussed how to manage first impressions. Leaving a position is your chance to make a parting shot and go out on top!

In any given week, I have several clients who are interviewing up/out, preparing an exit strategy, or longing for retirement. I am reminded of Blake, a senior director of product design in San Francisco, who says he's counting the days until he can exit his company. He says, "I've just got to stick it out for two more years," in what he describes as a toxic work environment. He dreams of leaving and going to a smaller startup. But for now, he is making the conscious choice to forgo other opportunities a little longer so that he can capitalize on the equity.

Sometimes people aren't quite ready to leave, but they know they need some time to pause and hit the refresh button. I am reminded of Susan, who has been climbing the ladder at the same consulting firm for 25 years. For the past year she has been reporting to a new executive who is questioning her value, which is giving her incredible anxiety. Truth be told, she is miserable and wants a fresh start, but she is scared to leave the only thing she knows. A couple of months ago, she hit her tipping point and had what can be described as a nervous breakdown. She is now two months into a company-sponsored leave of absence, spending her time and money on luxury travel, with hopes to return in the next month recharged and ready to work.

Blake and Susan both know that they are nearing the end of their time at their respective organizations. This is normal. Every job, just like every human relationship, comes to an end. Sometimes the end is involuntary (e.g., breakup, termination, or death). Other times it is voluntary. Just as an interview is often a first impression, the departure is our parting shot. For many people, it is the final way *they* remember you. And even beyond altruistic reasons for parting well, you never know when you will need that memory of you to be a positive and favorable one.

So regardless of the nature of your departure from a workplace, it is best to plan for saying goodbye well. Unless there are unusual circumstances to consider, here are some guidelines for how to communicate your way out of a job:

- **Submit your formal resignation when the time is right.** In general, this will be after your background check at the new job has cleared.

- **Tell your manager first.** Do it face-to-face or over a video call.

- **Avoid all urges to let the conversation take a negative turn.** Remember that you are not required to provide an explanation for why you are leaving. So this is not your time to blast anyone or the company at large. Unless you have a kind word that you'd like to share and have remembered, keep it short and sweet. Even if you are asked if there is something causing you to leave, do not feel obligated to take the bait. You can keep the focus of the conversation on those things that are good and positive. Highlight your desire to grow as a professional or pursue an opportunity for personal reasons.

- **Provide a minimum of two weeks' notice.** If you have lasted all this time, you can make it two more weeks. And be prepared to develop and deliver a quality transition plan. A proper transition is tangible evidence that you intend only good things for your soon-to-be former employer.

- **Express gratitude whenever possible.** Whether walking away from a toxic relationship or work environment, you can always be grateful for the learnings that led you to the point of leaving. Even in the worst of circumstances, you could say:

  > "Thank you all. I am so very grateful for the time here, as I know that the lessons learned will carry with me for many years to come."

ESSENTIAL TAKEAWAYS

- To partner with someone in solving a problem, you must describe the problem through a shared perspective.

- By coming to a partnership with a shared commitment and agreed on goals and objectives, you will strengthen your professional bonds while tackling issues and avoiding unnecessary conflict.

- If you approach potential conflict with a collaborative and compromising mindset, you can harness the conflict for good, leading to higher-quality outcomes and stronger bonds.

- Beware of the "Four Horsemen" of poor communication: criticism, defensiveness, contempt, and stonewalling.

- We can be people who have difficult conversations, disagreements even, but still commit to the people and the success of the group. Doing so is how savvy communicators protect their personal and professional relationships, which are essential for living a successful and satisfying life.

- Express gratitude whenever possible. Whether you are walking away from a toxic relationship or work environment, you can always be grateful for the learnings that led you to the point of leaving.

CHAPTER

17

Continue Learning to Keep Improving

Throughout this book, we have explored the communication essentials; learned how to apply the star framework for effective communication across myriad professional interactions; and gained implementable tools and strategies for navigating how to communicate into a job, out of one, and everything in between. In this final chapter, I trust you will conclude that communicating is a critical life skill, like eating or sleeping, that you can always be improving. Having a firm grasp of the essentials outlined in this book and applying them daily will position you to become a best-in-class communicator.

The critical next steps in your journey are to be gracious and continue learning.

First, be gracious to others because chances are they are humans who, like you, are doing the best they can with the cards they've been dealt. So, if you've got an annoying colleague who sends miserably long emails that seem to lack a purpose, you have choices. You can roll your eyes and move on with your day. You can respond matter-of-factly (e.g., *I'm confused. What is this?*). Or you could be a bit more gracious, assume best intent, and then go the extra mile. Perhaps give him a call or visit and say something like this:

> "Hey, I appreciate you making the time to provide all this information, but honestly, I'm struggling to make sense of it. I'd love to get a better sense of what I am supposed to do with your email. As well, if you have the time and are interested, I'd gladly share some email tricks that I have learned, which have helped me and could potentially help you."

When your colleague takes you up on your offer, you'd obviously share some pro tips from this book (e.g., the *what, so what, now what* framework described in Chapter 14). Now, it's possible that your colleague may dismiss you, but that's on that person. Your opportunity here is to be a good colleague who communicates effectively and hopes to help others do the same.

Another example of how you can be a gracious communicator and champion others is to look out for those who may be struggling to find their voice in meetings. You will recall from Chapter 3 that each of our communication styles has been impacted by our water jug, which is filled with the experiences and the memorable messages we have received throughout life. Within your professional network, there may be any number of individuals whose water jugs are a little muddy. Perhaps they've received some ugly or painful messages that are preventing them from communicating their best. You can be the one that helps, by encouraging them to speak (e.g., "Lauren, I'd love to know your thoughts, if you'd be willing to share") and affirming their efforts to do so (e.g., signaling support nonverbally by strong eye contact, nodding your head, and perhaps even smiling). They may not love being put on the spot, but your interest in their thoughts and your non-verbal affirmations can have an incredible impact.

Communicating grace and championing others has potential to impact other people for good. It also has a high probability of making you feel good about yourself. But there are two additional benefits worth mentioning. First, every time you share your knowledge of the communication essentials with others, you are also relearning them for yourself. Second, when you champion someone else, you are more likely to make or deepen a relationship with that person, which is a critically important step toward enhancing your brand in the workplace.

That being said, while you are busy championing fellow communicators and extending grace to them, be sure to do the same for yourself. On days when I go for a long run and can hardly finish my route, it's easy to feel defeated, like something is wrong with me. But when doing so, I fail to remember that there was a day when I could hardly run at all! The same can be true for elevating your communication skills. Eventually, it becomes second nature. And then one day, you trip over yourself during a meeting, get called out for a poorly worded memo, or maybe even bomb an interview. This doesn't mean that all is lost.

As a strong communicator, when you experience a momentary blip, it's not a sign that you have fallen; it's more a sign of how high you have climbed! For example, I have this conversation regularly with Charlie, a vice president of marketing, who has been a client of mine for years. When we first met, his confidence as a communicator was at zero. Extremely intelligent and ready to excel in his role, he still second-guessed every email, struggled at leading team meetings, and sweated calls with senior leaders and clients. Within a few months of extensive work together, Charlie had become an extremely capable and confident communicator. He was promoted, his team was expanded, and he was receiving regular feedback from his manager and C suite about how impressed people were with him. I started hearing from him less frequently, which I took to be a good sign.

Then a couple of months went by, and I got a text that read, *We gotta talk!* For the next two hours, I listened and consoled, and then we hatched a plan going forward. The big issue was that no one was complimenting him anymore! Well, of course, they weren't; his newfound communication skills weren't surprising anyone anymore. He had established a new baseline standard that people now held him against.

This is a cautionary tale of what happens when you elevate your skills and people come to expect you to deliver as an effective communicator. When I met Charlie, he was reaching out for help because he was striking out regularly in his communications. Within months, he was hitting communication home runs consecutively. Just as he readjusted as a communicator, those in his professional network readjusted their expectations of him as a communicator. Now, a home run might get a high five and a base hit is hardly noticed.

As you elevate your communication skills, know that you will miss some shots and maybe even lose a game. That's OK. Be gracious with yourself and just keep learning. I've heard a plethora of communication stories, some humorous and others not, from clients and friends who've learned some lessons the hard way. There is the one about the job applicant who was in a rush to get home following her interview and unknowingly cut off (and flipped off) the hiring manager on the interstate. There is the one about the guy who left his promotion meeting, called his college buddy while on the toilet, and detailed all the reasons he was shocked to have gotten the promotion. Of greatest shock to him was that no one knew he was hungover during the meeting. Of course, the joke was on him when he stepped out to wash his hands and found his manager waiting for him at the sink. Remember: you are always in presentation mode until you are home with the door shut and locked.

There will be moments when you know you could have done better and communicated more effectively. I encounter them regularly. The important thing is to examine your mishap through the lens of the communication essentials, and then brush yourself off and get back out there! This is what it means to be a communication student for life.

We must keep learning, growing, evolving, and chasing after that best version of ourselves. The good news is that—no matter your age, position, or life story thus far—each of us can continue to enhance our communication effectiveness. I wrote this book to provide more people with the communication essentials for winning in the workplace and beyond. If you don't understand and apply the communication essentials, you leave yourself vulnerable to unnecessary failure.

The communication essentials I've described in this book will enable you to express yourself and your ideas better, elevate your career, and bring you joy and satisfaction from making and maintaining meaningful relationships. But mastering the essentials is still no cause for a premature victory dance. While there may be some wins along the way, the learning never stops. It's all a journey, and the view gets better as you keep hiking upward.

So I implore you to be a communication student for life, not only for the joy of it, but also because new challenges are sure to arise. Part of what makes the communication learning journey challenging is that our personal and professional lives tend to become more complicated with age. For some of us, especially during our working years, this means the stakes grow higher as we get older. Sending a careless email to your professor in your freshman year of college may not be as consequential as sending a poorly worded memo to your CEO. Failing to meet your sales quota in your high school retail job may not cause the same career insecurity as making it to partner in a consulting firm but failing to win new business.

In addition to the stakes rising, our tools for communicating continue to evolve at breakneck speed. While this can be exciting, it often results in increasing the demands for communicators to always be on and respond immediately, especially as the demand for juggling multiple time zones, platforms, and devices fluently is only increasing. Challenges like these require us to be gracious and stay humble. We would be wise to be gracious with ourselves along the learning journey, and to extend that grace to others also.

Likewise, a bit of humility will encourage us to be nimble, adapt when beneficial, and demonstrate a willingness to learn and grow. And, lastly, although change will come and teach us new things, we must always keep a pivot foot on the communication essentials.

ESSENTIAL TAKEAWAYS

- Remember: you are always in presentation mode until you are home with the door shut and locked.

- Keep learning, growing, evolving, and chasing after a better version of yourself—no matter your age, position, or life story thus far.

- Although there may be some wins along the way, learning should never stop.

- Be gracious, stay humble, and extend that grace to others; be nimble, adapt when it's beneficial to do so; and be willing to learn and grow.

Notes

Chapter 1

1. Duck, S. W. *Meaningful Relationships: Talking, Sense, and Relating.* Thousand Oaks, CA: Sage Publications, 1994.

Chapter 2

1. Watzlawick, P., J. Beavin Bavelas, & D. D. Jackson. *Pragmatics of Human Communication: A Study of Interactional Patterns, Pathologies, and Paradoxes.* London: W.W. Norton, 1988.
2. Pietromonaco, P. R., & N. L. Collins. "Interpersonal Mechanisms Linking Close Relationships to Health," *American Psychologist.* U.S. National Library of Medicine, September 2017. https://pubmed.ncbi.nlm.nih.gov/28880100/.

Chapter 3

1. Jenkins, R. *Social Identity.* New York: Routledge, 2014.

Chapter 4

1. Brody, J. E. "Personal Health," *New York Times*, August 19,1992. https://www.nytimes.com/1992/08/19/health/personal-health-922392.html.

Chapter 6

1. Seinfeld, J. *Is This Anything?* New York: Simon & Schuster, 2020.
2. Dweck, C. S. *Mindset: The New Psychology of Success.* New York: Random House, 2006.

Chapter 8

1. Kennedy, T. "Faith, Truth and Tolerance in America," Liberty Baptist College, filmed October 3, 1983. https://www.Americanrhetoric.com/speeches/tedkennedytruth&tolerance.htm.
2. Gehrke, P. J., W. M. Keith, D. Beard, & G. Bodie. "Listening Research in the Communication Discipline," in *A Century of Communication Studies: The Unfinished Conversation.* New York: Routledge, Taylor & Francis Group, 2015.
3. Brownell, J. (1994). "Teaching listening: Some thoughts on behavioral approaches," *Business Communication Quarterly*, 57, 19–24.

Chapter 9

1. Markels, A. (2006). "Turning the Tide at P&G," *US News*. Posted 10/22/06.

Chapter 10

1. Fullwood, C., & G. Doherty-Sneddon. (2006). "Effect of Gazing at the Camera During a Video Link on Recall," *Applied Ergonomics*, 37(2), 167–175.
2. Conway, C. A., B. C. Jones, L. M. DeBruine, & A. C. Little. (2008). "Evidence for Adaptive Design in Human Gaze Preference," *Proceedings. Biological Sciences*, 275(1630), 63–69. https://doi.org/10.1098/rspb.2007.1073.

Chapter 11

1. McLuhan, M., & Q. Fiore. (1967). "The Medium Is the Message," *New York*, 123(1), 126–128.

Chapter 13

1. Fang, L., G. A. van Kleef, & D. A. Sauter. (2018). "Person perception from changing emotional expressions: Primacy, recency, or averaging effect?," *Cognition & Emotion*, 32, 1597–1610.
2. Bergeron, J., J. M. Fallu, & J. Roy. (2008). "A comparison of the effects of the first impression and the last impression in a selling context," *Recherche et Application en Marketing*, 23, 19–36.

Chapter 15

1. Guinn, T. (2016). "Friendship Work," *About Campus*, 20(6), 23–26. https://doi.org/10.1002/abc.21221.
2. Segrin, C., & S. A. Passalacqua. (2010). "Functions of loneliness, social support, health behaviors, and stress in association with poor health," *Health Communication*, 25(4), 312–322. https://doi.org/10.1080/10410231003773334.
3. Thibaut, J. W., & H. H. Kelley. *The Social Psychology of Groups.* New York: John Wiley & Sons, 1959.
4. Walster, E., E. Berscheid, & G. W. Walster. (1973). "New directions in equity research," *Journal of Personality and Social Psychology*, 25(2), 151–176. https://doi.org/10.1037/h0033967.
5. Stafford, L. (2011). "Measuring relationship maintenance behaviors: Critique and development of revised relationship maintenance behavioral scale," *Journal of Social and Personal Relationships*, 28, 278–303.

Chapter 16

1. Hocker, J. L., & W. W. Wilmot. *Interpersonal Conflict* (11th ed.). New York: McGraw Hill, 2022.
2. Guinn, T. (2018). "Two Action Items for Building Consensus and Improving Workplace Relationships," *The Department Chair*, 28(4), 6–7.
3. Gottman, J. M., & N. Silver. *The Seven Principles for Making Marriage Work.* New York: Harmony Books, 2015.
4. Horan, S. M., T. D. Guinn, & S. Banghart. (2015). "Understanding relationships among the dark triad personality profile and romantic partners' conflict communication," *Communication Quarterly*, 63(2), 156–170.
5. Lencioni, P. *The Advantage: Why Organizational Health Trumps Everything Else in Business.* San Francisco: Jossey-Bass, 2012.
6. Kantor, J., & D. Streitfeld. (2015). "Inside Amazon: Wrestling big ideas in a bruising workplace," *New York Times*, 15(08), 1–19.

Index

A

Accountability, for take five concept, 244

Action model, 17, 19, 24

Active listening, 230
  barriers to, 89–91
  to develop network, 160–161
  HURIER model for, 91–96
  for relationships, 187–188
  shared meaning from, 88–89
  to unspoken messages, 87

Advice, help compared to, 158, 176

"Agree to disagree," disagree and commit compared to, 247

Amazon (company), 208, 245

Anxiety, presentation, 55–56, 59–60

Apologies, habitual, 182

Appeal
  for compelling message, 112–113, 116, 119
  credibility as, 119, 125
  in sales pitch, 114–115

Asynchronous messaging, synchronous interaction compared to, 147

Attire
  communication through, 37–38
  preparation of, 72

Audience, 63, 79–83, 96, 100–101. *See also* Communication Star
  communication style adapted for, 192–193, 206

cover letter for specific, 161–162, 176
  description of, 66, 67
  goal relation to, 46–47, 84, 86–87
  message centered on, 104–106, 108, 116–117, 119, 139
  message medium relation to, 145, 146, 152
  vocal delivery connecting to, 131

Authenticity, confidence and, 125–126

Avoidance
  of communication pitfalls, 197–199
  of conflict, 229–230, 233–235, 236–237, 243, 245
  of criticism, 222, 225
  of miscommunication, 205, 214
  of negativity, 223, 225, 249

B

Bezos, Jeff, 208

Bieber, Justin, 144

Body language, verbal message relation to, 7

Brand, personal, 190–191, 202, 208
  avoiding negativity in, 223, 225
  championing others for, 253
  for climbing professional ladder, 189–190
  communication style to serve, 193–194
  in digital communication, 203–204
  talking points for, 198–200

Brody, Jane, 38–39

C

Career. *See also* Ladder, professional
  intoxication wrecking, 209–210
Cicero, Marcus, 81–82
Clarity
  filler words hindering, 128–129, 140
  of goal, 74–77
  of message, 70, 72, 74, 77, 98–99,
      101–102, 118
Closed-mindedness, as barrier to
    listening, 90
Collaborative communication, 19
Colleagues, empathy for, 205–206
Communication. *See specific topics*
Communication Star, 55
  five points of, 62–68
Competence, confidence relation to,
    123–125
Composition, of written
    communication, 208–209
Confidence, 122–125
  behaviors that betray, 126–127
  in delivery, 127–128, 139
  pause relation to, 130–131
Conflict, 227–230, 232, 242, 247
  avoidance of, 233–235, 236–237,
      243, 245
  destructive behaviors in, 237–241,
      244
  frustration relation to, 236
Consensus
  problem statement for, 232, 234–235
  before solution, 231–233
Contempt, from negativity, 240
Context, shared meaning relation to, 23
Core messaging, in interviews, 163–164
Cover letter, specific audience in,
    161–162, 176
Credibility, 63
  as appeal, 119, 125
  delivery relation to, 140

  establishment of, 185, 194–195
  vocal fillers diminishing, 129–130
Criticism
  avoidance of, 222, 225
  as destructive conflict behavior,
      237–238
Cultural norms, 8–9, 13
  of eye contact, 134
  of first impressions, 178–179

D

Daly, John, 158, 186
Decoder/Receiver, 21
Defensive thinking, offensive compared
    to, 30–34
DEI. *See* Diversity, equity, inclusion
Delivery
  competence relation to, 123–125
  confidence in, 127–128, 139
  credibility relation to, 140
  energy infused through, 137–138
  rehearsal of, 122–123
  of story in interview, 170–172
  visual, 132–133
  vocal, 127–128, 131, 132–133
Departure, from workplace, 247–249
Difficult conversations, 227–228, 236.
    See also Conflict
  savvy communicators having, 247,
      250
Digital communication, 205. *See also*
    Email; Social media
  first impressions in, 204
  norms in, 206–207
  personal brand in, 203–204
  stonewalling in, 241
Disagree and commit
  "agree to disagree" compared to, 247
  as leadership principle, 245–246
Diversity, equity, inclusion (DEI), 5
Dweck, Carol, 58

E

Effectiveness, communication, 255
  confidence for, 126
  feedback loops for, 44–45, 48
  indicator of, 41–42
  inner work for, 25–26, 34
Ego, 242
  as obstacle, 115–116
  as "other goals," 74–76
  simple messaging and, 102
Email
  as message medium, 142
  norms for, 207
  tone of, 85
Emotion, in messaging, 115–116
Empathy, for colleagues, 205–206
Energy, delivery infusing, 137–138
Equity, in relationships, 221–222,
    224–225
Evaluation, fear of, 58–59
Executive presence
  development of, 192–193
  in meetings, 194–195
Expectations, about message medium,
    149–151, 152
Eye contact, 135–136, 140
  cultural cues from, 134
  feedback from, 138
  memory relation to, 133
  verbal message relation to, 7

F

Facial expression, verbal message
    relation to, 7
Fear
  of communicating, 59–60
  of evaluation, 58–59
Feedback, 60
  dismissal of, 42–43, 48
  from eye contact, 138
  loops, 44–45, 48

Filler words
  clarity hindered by, 128–129, 140
  credibility diminished by, 129–130
First impressions. *See also* Primacy
    effect
  cultural norms of, 178–179
  in digital communication, 204
  in introductions, 185–186, 202
  in promotion, 180–182
"Four Horsemen" of poor
    communication, 250
  contempt as, 240–241
  criticism as, 237–238
  defensiveness as, 239–240
  stonewalling as, 241–242
Framework, communication, 214
  recap, request, and remind, 210–212
  what, so what, now what, 212–213,
    252
  what, why, how, 195–197, 202
Friendship work, for network, 215,
    219, 222
Frustration, conflict relation to,
    228–229, 236
Funnel structure, pyramid compared
    to, 106–108, 119

G

Gestures, rehearsal of, 132
Gettysburg Address (Lincoln), 6
Glazing over, as barrier to listening, 90
Goal(s), 9. *See also* Communication Star
  audience relation to, 46–47, 79–81,
    84, 86–87
  clarity of, 74–77
  communication, 16, 24, 46–47
  conflict in incompatible, 229–230
  ego needs as, 74–76
  message medium relation to, 146, 152
  preparation relation to, 69, 70–73,
    76, 77

Goal(s), *(cont'd)*
    refinement of, 67
    shared meaning as, 23
Gottman, John, 237
Grace, in communication, 252–256

H

Help, advice compared to, 158, 176
Human connection, 4
Humility
    in adaptation, 256
    in interview, 163–164, 168
HURIER model, for active listening,
    91–96

I

Idea, as solution, 116–117
Identity, communication expressing,
    16, 24
Impact, intentions versus, 45–46
Information overload
    as barrier to listening, 90
    in message, 99–100
Inner work, for communication
    effectiveness, 25–26, 34
Insecurities, as obstacle, 74–76
Intentions, impact versus, 45–46
Interaction model, 18, 19–20, 24
Internal messaging, norms for, 206
Interview
    anxiety in, 56
    core messaging in, 163–165
    cover letter securing, 161–162
    power dynamics in, 44
    preparation for, 227–228
    questions in, 168–170, 173–175
    story told in, 170–172
    tone in, 166–168, 175
    transaction model in, 20
Intoxication, wrecking career, 209–210
Intrapersonal messages, 27–29

Introductions, first impressions in,
    185–186, 204
Invitations
    for initiating relationships, 220
    to personal network, 224
Isolation, from network, 218

J

Job search. *See also* Interview
    language in, 162–163
    using network in, 157–158, 176, 216

K

Kennedy, Ted, 84

L

Ladder, professional
    network to climb, 161
    personal brand for climbing, 189–190
Lafley, A.G., on messages, 102
Language, 182
    analogous, 102–103
    confidence betrayed by, 126–127
    filler words in, 128–130, 140
    of résumé, 162–163
Leadership principle, disagree and
    commit as, 245–246
Learning journey, 3–4, 255
Liberty Baptist College, 84
Life experiences, effect on
    communication, 26–30
Lincoln, Abraham, 6
LinkedIn, job search on, 157
Listening. *See* Active listening

M

Main point, in messaging, 109–111
Meanings, messages and, 9–12, 13
Memory
    eye contact relation to, 133
    message medium relation to, 143

Message, 65–66, 68, 138–139, 212.
See also Communication Star;
Language
analogous language in, 102–103
appeals for compelling, 112–115,
116, 119
audience centered, 100–101, 104–106,
108, 116–117, 119
clarity of, 70, 72, 74, 77, 98–99,
101–102, 118
core of, 195–196
information overload in, 99–100
meanings and, 9–12, 13
as message medium, 141–143, 148,
152
pyramid structure for, 109–112, 116,
210
recap, 205, 214
staying on, 197–198, 202
structure of, 106–112, 214
timing of, 63
verbal, 7
Message medium, 21–22, 24, 62–63, 67,
85, 147. See also Communication
Star
audience relation to, 145, 146, 152
in communication style, 150–151
expectations about, 149–151, 152
goal relation to, 146, 152
message as, 141–143, 148, 152
virtual environments as, 144–146
Messenger, 62–63. See also
Communication Star
confidence of, 123–124
preparation of, 122–123
Metaphor, in messaging, 102–104
Mindset, fixed versus growth, 58
Miscommunication, 36–37
recap message to avoid, 205, 214
Muted responses, as "Netflix face,"
136–137

N

Negativity
avoidance of, 223, 225, 249
as communication pitfall, 223, 225
contempt from, 240
in self-talk, 27–29
"Netflix face," muted responses as,
136–137
Network, 159–161
avoiding negativity in, 223
friendship work for, 215, 219, 222
invitations to, 224
isolation from, 218
job search using, 157–158, 176, 216
New York Times (newspaper), 38–39
Noise, 21–22
as barrier to listening, 89
Nonverbal communication, 23–24, 29
accuracy in, 38–39
confidence in, 127
Norms
cultural, 8–9, 13, 134, 178–179
in digital communication, 206–207

O

Obama, Barack, 144
Obstacle
ego as, 115–116
insecurities as, 74–76
Offensive thinking, defensive compared
to, 30–34
One-way communication, 17
Opinions, formation of, 37–38

P

Pandemic, relationships during, 15,
217–219
Pauses, 140
confidence relation to, 130–131
Performance evaluation
goal clarity for, 75–76
standard rubric for, 115

Phone call, courtesy in, 85
Physical proximity, in relationships, 219
Physiological arousal, 59–60
Pitfalls, communication
    avoidance of, 197–199
    negativity as, 223
    talking points to avoid, 201, 202
Position, in effective communication, 45
Positivity, communication of, 222–223
Power dynamics, feedback relation to, 43–44
Preparation, 98. *See also* Rehearsal
    of attire, 72
    goals relation to, 69, 70–73, 76, 77
    for interview, 227–228
    of messenger, 122–123
    quality of, 61
    of talking points, 197–200
Presentation
    anxiety in, 55–56
    mode for, 254–255, 256
    of résumé, 156
Presentational communication, representational compared to, 155–156
Primacy effect. *See also* First impressions
    recency effect compared to, 182–183
Problem statement
    for consensus, 232, 234–235
    shared meaning in, 250
Promotion, first impressions in, 180–182
Proposal, well-formulated, 117–118
Pseudo-listening, as barrier to listening, 90
Public speaking
    anxiety from, 56
    physiological arousal from, 59

Pyramid structure
    funnel compared to, 106–108, 119
    for messaging, 109–112, 116, 210

Q

Quantitative evidence, in *what, why, how* structure, 196–197
Questions, in interview, 168–170, 173–175

R

Rebuttal
    as barrier to listening, 90
    refuting, 117–118, 119
Recap, request, and remind framework, 210–212, 214
Recency effect, primacy effect compared to, 182–183
Rehearsal. *See also* Preparation
    of delivery, 122–123
    of gestures, 132
Relational norms, communication style accommodating, 8–9, 13
Relationships, 9, 247–249
    active listening for, 187–188
    championing others in, 252–253
    communication skills in, 217
    conflict in, 236–237
    equity in, 221–222, 224–225
    invitations initiating, 220
    during pandemic, 15, 217–219
    physical proximity in, 219
    strong ties in, 186–187
Representational communication, presentational compared to, 155–156
Resignation letter, 249
Résumé, 156
    in interview, 163–165
    language of, 162–163

S

Sales pitch, appeal in, 114–115
Savvy communicators
    audience centered approach of, 80,
        87, 206
    eye contact of, 135
    goals of, 76
    having difficult conversations, 247,
        250
    message medium choice of, 143
    presentational communication of,
        156
Seinfeld, Jerry, 56
Self-Assessment, Communication,
    51–54
Self-compassion, 29–30
Self-talk, negative, 27–29
Sender, of message, 21
Shared meaning, 23
    from active listening, 88–89
    in problem statement, 250
Simultaneous communication, 18
Skills, communication, 39
    elevation of, 112, 254
    for forming connections,
        219–225
    life success linked to, 48
    in relationships, 217
Social exchange theory, equity in,
    221–222
Social media. *See also* Digital
    communication
    LinkedIn as, 157
    as message medium, 147
    presentational communication in,
        156
    Twitter as, 144
Solution
    consensus before, 231–233
    idea as, 116–117
Story, told in interview, 170–172

Strengths, in brand development,
    190–192
Structure
    in interview, 166–168, 175
    of message, 106–112, 116, 119,
        196–197, 210, 214
Student, of communication, 3–4, 255
Style, communication, 8–9, 13
    adaptation of, 192–194, 206
    message medium in, 150–151
Synchronous interactions,
    asynchronous messaging
    compared to, 147

T

Take five concept, for conflict
    avoidance, 243
    accountability for, 244
Talking points, 197–200
    to avoid pitfalls, 201, 202
Technology, communication, evolution
    of, 5, 12
Thank-you card, to network, 159
Timing, of message, 63
Tone
    of email, 85
    in interview, 166–168, 175
Tools, communication. *See also*
    Message medium
    grace using, 256
Transaction model, 18–20, 24
Twitter, as message medium, 144

U

Unspoken messages, active listening
    to, 87

V

Values
    brand expressing, 190, 202
    conflict avoided by shared, 229–230

Verbal message, body language relation to, 7

Virtual environments, as message medium, 144–146. *See also* Social media

Visual delivery, vocal relation to, 132–133

Visuals, dynamic contrasted with static, 6–7

Vocal delivery, 131
confidence in, 127–128
visual relation to, 132–133

W

What, so what, now what framework, 212–213, 214, 252

What, why, how framework, 195–197, 202

Willingness, 60
to improve, 56–57, 58–59
to speak, 68

Written communication. *See also* Digital communication; Email
care in, 207–208
composition of, 208–209

About the Author

 **Trey Guinn** is a professor and department chair of Communication Arts at University of the Incarnate Word. He is also a business communication specialist for The University of Texas at Austin and communication coach with the McCombs School of Business. His teaching, research, and professional work focus primarily on communication effectiveness and human relationships.

As a speaker, facilitator, and executive coach, Trey helps people achieve personal and professional goals and master communication skills. He frequently works with groups and professionals locally and across the globe from companies such as American Express, Apple, AT&T, Bain, BBVA-Compass, BCG, Chevron, Dell, Deloitte, Facebook, GE, Harvard Business School, Hewlett-Packard, Intel, Intuit, McKinsey, Microsoft, PWC, Salesforce, Shell, Snap, and more.

Trey earned his bachelor's and master's degrees from Baylor University and his PhD from The University of Texas at Austin. His scholarship has been presented and published internationally. He remains actively involved with numerous academic organizations, and currently serves as president of the Fulbright Association–San Antonio chapter.

An award-winning actor, Trey is also an avid runner and kitchen experimenter. Most importantly, he is the husband of Shannon and the dad of three incredible kids. The Guinns reside in Alamo Heights, Texas, where they can often be spotted walking the neighborhood and playing in the park.

McGraw Hill's NEW Business Essentials Series delivers must-know info and action steps for topics every business professional needs to succeed in today's new world of work

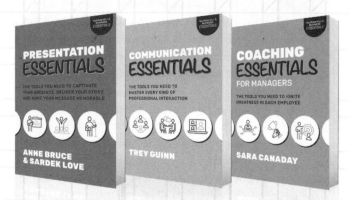

Filled with colored illustrations, assessments, toolkits, action steps, and more, readers will walk away from each book in the Business Essentials Series feeling fully prepared to put their sharpened skills into action right away, even if they never received formal training in that area before!

Organized in three easy-to-digest sections—The Essentials, The Essentials Applied, and Beyond the Essentials—each title in the series shows readers how they can excel in different areas of business from leadership and coaching, all the way to presenting and communicating—in person, online, or a combination of the two.